D1236158

Madness and Reason

Studies in Applied Philosophy
edited by *Brenda Cohen* and *Anthony O'Hear*

Madness and Reason

Jennifer Radden

Department of Philosophy,
University of Massachusetts

London
GEORGE ALLEN & UNWIN
Boston   Sydney

George Allen & Unwin (Publishers) Ltd,
40 Museum Street, London WC1A 1LU, UK

George Allen & Unwin (Publishers) Ltd,
Park Lane, Hemel Hempstead, Herts HP2 4TE, UK

Allen & Unwin Inc.,
8 Winchester Place, Winchester, Mass 01890, USA

George Allen & Unwin Australia Pty Ltd,
8 Napier Street, North Sydney, NSW 2060, Australia

First published in 1985

British Library Cataloguing in Publication Data

Radden, Jennifer
   Madness and reason.—(Studies in applied philosophy)
1. Mental health   2. Psychology—Philosophy
I. Title II. Series
613   RA790
ISBN 0-04-170034-1
ISBN 0-04-170035-X Pbk

Library of Congress Cataloging in Publication Data

Radden, Jennifer.
  Madness and reason.
(Studies in applied philosophy;)
Bibliography: p.
Includes index.
1. Ethics. 2. Irrationalism (Philosophy) 3. Mental illness—Moral
and ethical aspects. I. Title. II. Series.
BJ45.R33 1985   170   85-7489
ISBN 0-04-170034-1 (U.S. : alk. paper)
ISBN 0-04-170035-X (U.S. : pbk. : alk. paper)

Set in 11 on 12 point Garamond by Paston Press, Norwich
and printed in Great Britain by Biddles Ltd, Guilford, Surrey

Editors' Preface

Studies in Applied Philosophy is intended to provide a focus for
philosophical work which makes a positive and constructive
contribution to contemporary debates in many areas of public
life. In law, politics, economics, science, medicine and education,
issues arise which have both ethical and philosophical dimensions.
Each author approaches such issues from the critical and reflective
standpoint characteristic of philosophy. The series is based on the
belief that such an approach need not imply either moral ambivalence or an unwillingness to draw conclusions, and authors will
in general defend a position and point of view. However, the
purpose of the series will equally be served if a contribution
provokes controversy or widespread assent.

Each volume will be of interest to students and teachers involved
in academic and professional courses who wish to examine the
philosophical and ethical assumptions made in their particular
fields. At the same time, the series will interest students and
teachers of philosophy who would like to see their own discipline
provide a serious and constructive approach to matters of practical concern. By avoiding unnecessary technicalities, but without
sacrificing rigour of argument, the books will also be accessible to
the concerned general reader whose life is touched by the decisions of politicians and professionals, and who wishes to clarify
the ethical arguments used or avoided in this process. We believe
that *Studies in Applied Philosophy* will be of interest to all those
concerned with the philosophical issues underlying debate and
decision-making.

Brenda Cohen
Anthony O'Hear

To M. B. Radden,
my mother

Acknowledgements

I am grateful to many people for help and inspiration with this book – my friends and colleagues, my social work clients and philosophy students. I would particularly like to acknowledge John Fordyce, who first roused my interest in the M'Naghten's Rule in Australia during the 1960s, and those who have read and helped with earlier drafts of my manuscript: Ann Diller, Jane Martin, Susan Fransoza, Janet Farrell Smith, Barbara Houston, Howard Cohen, Lawrence Foster, Brad Honoroff, Owen Flannagan, Margaret Rhodes, R. K. Shope and Frank Keefe.

I am especially grateful to these last three: Margaret Rhodes has provided unfailing encouragement and ideas since the project's inception; Bob Shope undertook a painstaking and careful reading of the final draft; and my husband Frank Keefe has offered moral support and philosophical and editorial comment for the several years that this work has been in the making. Whatever shortcomings remain are entirely mine.

Finally, I would like to thank Ann Hegyi for practical help without which the book would never have been completed.

Contents

1
Madness and Moral Responsibility

Introduction

It is widely agreed that insanity serves as an excuse. The issue explored here is not whether but why it should.

An impulse or moral intuition to excuse the insane wrongdoer lacks adequate theoretical grounding or justification today, I would argue, due to two developments in the way madness has been understood in the twentieth century. One is the adoption and entrenchment of a medical model in which madness is seen as analogous to physical disease. The other, paradoxically, is the anti-psychiatry movement which arose as an explicit reaction to the influence of that model.

One of the most vivid reflections of this problem is found in law relating to insanity which has been subjected to an increasing medical influence at both a theoretical and a procedural level, with the adoption in the influential Durham Rule of a blanket medical classification to distinguish the sane from the insane wrongdoer and with the courtroom practice of abdicating responsibility for legal decisions about insanity to clinicians in their role as expert witnesses.

Moreover, the influences of the medical model and of the anti-psychiatry movement have together brought about the eclipse of an earlier analysis of madness to which appeal could be made in grounding the moral intuition to excuse: madness construed as a form of irrationality or 'unreason', analogous to the exculpating want of reason we acknowledge in children.

The central proposal of this book is that we must recover the earlier conception of madness as unreason in order to justify and ground our important conviction that madness is an excuse.[1]

Due to the influences of the medical model and anti-psychiatry, but also, perhaps, to the very obviousness of the equation between sanity and reason, which has invited its trivialization, the thesis that madness is a want of reason has been overlooked. Even the tradition of analytic philosophy in which this work is placed, has contributed to its neglect. Philosophers have consistently disregarded madness in their discussions of irrationality. They have accepted the standard view that analyses in terms of a want of reason fail to capture the vagaries of madness [see Fingarette (1967), Boorse (1975), Flew (1975) and, more recently, Culver and Gert (1982)], and they have adopted too readily the prevailing medical conception of it.

There are several significant exceptions to this generalization, however, and these deserve mention. Feinberg (1970) has explored the notion that certain neurotic disorders might be characterized in terms of a particular kind of irrationality and, while he was concerned with conditions less severe than those which I discuss, his work stimulated my own interest in this area. More recently, Edwards (1982) – with his model of mental health as rational autonomy – and Moore (1975, 1980) have both proposed the neglected thesis that irrationality accounts for the exculpating nature of severe derangement although neither author has acknowledged the seriousness of the challenges to that claim – challenges, in my view, to which a response must be offered before it can be maintained.

Both a critique and a positive proposal are set forth here. The analogy with disease underlying the medical view of madness is found wanting, particularly as it is reflected in contemporary legal trends, and so also are certain tenets of anti-psychiatry. Positively, I urge that we return to the earlier notion of madness as unreason which could serve to ground our impulse to excuse the insane.

The positive thesis that madness is unreason and that unreason counts to exculpate, rests on three points. First, appeal is made to a sixteenth- and seventeenth-century conception of madness derived from Foucault's work (1961, 1963) where it is suggested that between the Renaissance and the Age of Reason, a shift occurred in the nature of insanity and the way it was understood. From being unreason (*déraison*) and viewed as a form of illogicality or unreasonableness allied to the ordinary, imperfectly rational thought of sane people, it came to be madness (*folie*) and to be seen as a medical condition and as – in certain respects – removed, remote and inexplicable. The earlier structure, in which madness was unreason, is the one from which my analysis is derived.

Secondly, the thesis that mad people are less rational or reasonable – that they exhibit unreason – is defended. The variety of claims associated with the use of the terms 'rational', 'irrational' and 'reasonable' are explored, thereby explaining the force of Foucault's term 'unreason'. It is shown how the thesis is confirmed in the paradigms of derangement – schizophrenia and other psychotic states. Moreover, it is argued that even in cases of severe derangement seemingly recalcitrant to such an unreason analysis – like paranoia and affective disorders – a closer examination reveals that there are particular patterns of perceiving and feeling in each which must be expected to lead to irrationally held beliefs and desires and to errors of judgement.

Thirdly, it is shown that, since strong parallels link the want of reason exhibited by the insane and children alike, the same principle of exculpating nonrationality found in juvenile law can be appealed to in grounding our intuition to excuse the insane. It is, then, because of their unreason that we want to exonerate the insane.

Next, the question of the normativism endemic to any account of madness is addressed. The 'irrationality' of madness when that term merely connotes deviance is unremarkable. It is necessary to go further and argue – as the term unreason suggests – that the insane are distinguished not merely by unusual responses but by defects of judgement.

Finally, the ramifications of my thesis for the legal notion of insanity are broached directly and suggestions are put forward as to legal procedures and practice which could overcome the problem raised at the outset: that our intuition to excuse the insane must be better grounded.

A few words are now required about the scope of the concept of madness and the terminology employed here, and finally about my own philosophical method.

When we speak loosely of mental aberration, we often evisage a spectrum of cases ranging from the most pervasive and severe derangement – sheer lunacy, or psychosis – at the one extreme to minor, specific, neurotic reactions like a faintly unusual or dysfunctional attitude towards love, or neatness or enclosed spaces, at the other. This conception is favoured by the mental health profession shaping the 'psychological society' (Gross, 1978) we inhabit at this end of the twentieth century. We may be sane, the platitude runs, but we are all a little neurotic. Mental health is as much an unreachable ideal as it is a state we might expect to find embodied in an actual person.

The minor neurotic conditions at the sane end of the spectrum, however, are of no importance to my thesis and will not be dealt with in this book. The concept of madness with which I am concerned is restricted to more severe afflictions: to psychotic states where reality testing is impaired, together with a small number of other conditions included because of the pervasiveness of their effect on the mind, personality or behaviour of their sufferer. Among psychotic conditions the most central are the schizophrenias and the severest forms of affective disorder, mania and depression. Among nonpsychotic conditions, I am concerned primarily with pervasive and serious manic and depressive reactions, and with the condition known as pure paranoia.

With the exception of the latter, nonpsychotic conditions and with the special case of compulsive behaviour, then, my thesis is not intended to cover what are classified as neurotic disorders, such as anxiety reactions, nor personality disorders like the obsessional personality.

This restriction is in keeping with the use of the word 'madness', it seems to me. The sufferers of anything less serious than the conditions described above may be mentally unhealthy, but we would hesitate to describe them as mad. More importantly, however, the restriction I have sketched roughly corresponds to a moral intuition: only the conditions I have named, it seems, are included in the widespread belief that mental derangement counts as an excuse for wrongdoing. Beyond these boundaries, evidence of the general agreement which marks the adoption of that moral stance is no longer present, either in technical or in lay discussions.[2]

Because the moral stance in which I am interested is not univocal over the less severe conditions, I shall say little about these states. It may be that there is a kind of irrationality or unreason to be found in such disorders, but whether or not this is so remains unimportant for my thesis, since about those conditions the impulse to excuse does not seem to be consistently felt.

Thus, while I have tried to use terms corresponding in their usage to the category of mental aberration with which I am concerned, my primary intention here is not to give a general characterization of madness; indeed, I am not convinced that such a general characterization would be possible or useful. Rather, my purpose is to explain why insanity excuses when it seems to do so.

The choice of terminology for the class of aberrant mental states described above, and for particular conditions within that class, was not an easy one. The sanitized vocabulary of the medical framework is inappropriate in a work taking issue with that model; we cannot speak of these conditions as mental ill health if the very analogy giving life to that expression is in question. Of the abusive, archaic and extreme alternatives which remain, I have chosen to speak of the states to which I refer as derangement, madness and insanity, indifferently – ignoring, in the case of the last term, the increasing specialization its meaning has acquired as a legal equivalent of 'criminally insane'. In making reference to particular conditions, I have used traditional psychiatric terminology. Such terminology, while not immune from the evils of labelling to which anti-psychiatry writers have rightly drawn attention, nor from implicit medical assumptions, is at least free from explicit appeal to the analogies with disease and illness shaping those assumptions.

Finally, some comment is required on the philosophical method and presuppositions found here.

It hardly needs remarking that the thesis of this book presupposes a view of human action whereby the ordinary, sane wrongdoer is rightly held responsible for his or her crime and punished on its account; it is an assumption, indeed, which is central to the Anglo–American legal tradition. However, I shall avoid offering a full account of voluntary action and agent responsibility. Instead, my focus – like Aristotle's in the *Nichomachean Ethics* – will be on the circumstances under which we are inclined to withhold blame for action and to offer excuses.

To understand better when and why we want to excuse the insane should be to understand better the positive notions of agency and freedom. Austin remarks in his *A Plea for Excuses* that Aristotle has been chidden wrongly for overlooking 'the real problem' of freedom, for 'In examining all the ways in which each action may not be "free", i.e. the cases in which it will not do to say simply "X did A" we may hope to dispose of that problem' (Austin, 1956–57, p. 180). Austin is at least correct, I would insist, in asserting that we are not required to confront the problem of agency directly. Although I do not share his confidence that an adequate analysis of excuses would make any positive account of agency unnecessary – indeed I point to the need for such an account in outlining how our moral intuitions concerning madness and responsibility might find ultimate justification – it is not one which it is necessary to undertake here.

My argument relies on certain beliefs or moral intuitions about madness and responsibility. These are appealed to in particular cases to determine whether legal excuses should be extended to a wrongdoer who is deranged. They are also introduced in an exploration of the reasons to favour one account of madness over another. So it is important to look more closely at them.

The expression 'moral intuition', while apt, is in certain respects a misleading one. Moral intuitions have sometimes been taken to connote reactions which are at once precognitive, unchanging and unjustifiable. In pointing to the impulse to excuse insane wrongdoers I wish to imply none of these features. These moral intuitions reflect judgements in the sense of considered conclusions and not mere immediate and unthinking reactions. Moreover, they may change. They depend on a certain view of madness. Were our view to change, so that we ceased to regard madness as the affliction of a helpless sufferer, then the intuitions themselves could be expected to diminish or disappear. Finally, these convictions are justifiable. Support for the intuition to excuse mad people who commit crimes can be found in a theory about excusing conditions – ignorance, compulsion and, I shall argue, unreason. We accept the particular judgement that this insane wrongdoer ought to be excused because we recognize the validity of the general principle that, for example, ignorance excuses.

In asserting that these moral intuitions are justifiable, however, I am not proposing that they ought to be adopted by everyone. Contrary beliefs about the insane are also held by some people and it is not my purpose to mount an attack on their views. The convictions I am concerned with are widespread, which is sufficient for my argument. While I share them, I draw attention to these beliefs in order to explore the relationship they bear to certain ideas about the nature of madness, not to defend them.

My use of Foucault's ideas also requires clarification, but I shall leave this until Chapter 4 when those ideas are introduced.

Beliefs About Madness and Moral Responsibility

The attitudes towards the insane which are fundamental to my analysis now require closer scrutiny. The belief that insanity is an excuse is one of several widespread – although not universal – beliefs about madness and responsibility which influence and in turn are influenced by how we see the mad person. These beliefs centre around our inclination to treat insane people differently from the sane on account of their affliction: to regard them as innocent victims and as at least partially blameless in a moral sense, or as less than fully culpable or accountable for what they do. Such attitudes are expressed in a passage by the great reformer Pinel (1806, pp. 323–4). Those who are 'mentally sick', as he describes the insane,

> far from being guilty persons who merit punishment, are . . . people whose miserable state deserves all the consideration due to suffering humanity

Because these attitudes are often inexactly expressed and are shared by people with differing perspectives, they are not easily formulated. However, we might begin with a loose attempt to fix them using the terminology of *blamelessness*. First, it is supposed that the mad person ought not to be blamed for having become, or for being, mad. Obvious as it seems today, this belief has not always been accepted, and it requires careful attention. Let us call it *Belief 1*, and for conciseness formulate it:

Belief 1: Madness is not blameworthy.

Secondly, it is supposed that the mad person ought not to be blamed for action taken as the result of his or her condition. If the action is occasioned by the madness, then it counts as an excuse, and we do not hold the agent to have been responsible for it – at all, or at least to the same extent – as we would someone who was sane. *Belief 2*, then, may be formulated:

Belief 2: Madness mitigates blame for wrongdoing.

A number of qualifications and elaborations immediately suggest themselves here. First, it must be emphasized that I claim neither exhaustiveness nor universality for these beliefs. There are other moral attitudes held towards the insane as well as these (for instance, the view that they ought to receive help for their suffering). The second of the two beliefs, moreover, is questioned today by many people and sometimes countered with the contrary conviction that concern for their human freedom and dignity dictates that the insane *ought* to be held responsible for their actions. These ideas are not unimportant, particularly now when they seem to be influencing legal thought.[3] However, they will not be dealt with here. My purpose, as I indicated earlier, is not to show that the two beliefs I have singled out ought to be accepted but to explore their relationship to other ideas about the nature of madness.

Secondly, it must be stressed that these attitudes express distinct beliefs. As we shall see in a later chapter, it has sometimes been supposed that blamelessness of the first kind entails that of the second, i.e. that to be excused from blame for a condition (*Belief 1*) entails being excused from blame for actions stemming from that condition (*Belief 2*).

The general principle underlying such reasoning appears to be that if one acts out of an unwanted visitation, then one cannot be held responsible for the action any more than one can be for the visitation. But this – on the face of things – is surely false. We blame people for acting in character when to do so is vicious, even though the forming of their character was something for which we do not hold them to have been responsible. We blame them for expressing and harbouring vicious emotions like resentment and hatred, for example, without blaming them for having initially experienced those emotions. Similarly, our bodily appetites are caused in us and are sometimes unwished for, yet we are usually held responsible when we act on them.[4] So being blameless in having come by a condition does not generally entail being blameless in acting from it and neither, I would insist, does it do so in this case.

My third point is a *caveat* about *Belief 1*. This belief expresses the view that *because the insane are seen as the unwitting victims of their state* – nobody, it is usually agreed, wants to become mad, nor knows how to invite madness – they are not rightly held responsible for falling prey to it. It seems to follow that if we knew more about madness, so that the power to predict and prevent its onset lay with those it afflicts, then we would no longer regard them as the blameless victims we do today.

Next, it must be emphasized that *Belief 2* expresses an appeal to justice, not to pragmatic considerations. Some people believe that the insane wrongdoer should not be punished because the efficacy of legal sanctions makes little sense for a person who cannot understand them, and this may be true. However, I am not concerned with the convictions derived from a consequentialist view of punishment. The belief considered here maintains that it would be *unjust* to blame the insane wrongdoer, regardless of the impracticality or practicality of doing so.

Finally, a qualification is required on *Belief 2*, which casts madness as excuse, for it is only when wrongdoing is committed as the result of it or because of it that madness excuses in this way. We do not want to excuse lunatics for their action if it connects in no way with the psychological states, or their effects, which constitute their madness. A person with paranoia has no excuse for burglary if it relates in no way to the beliefs and desires making up his or her delusions.

What is the exact force of the 'because'? In most action taken out of madness, the psychological states constituting part of that condition stand as something less than a complete cause of the subsequent behaviour. Feelings of worthlessness and despair do not alone bring about the depressed person's self-destructive action. Other beliefs and desires are involved which are not themselves part of his or her condition. Rather, the psychological states comprising the manifestations of insanity are *part* of the cause of the subsequent wrongdoing when we treat madness as an excuse. Two qualifications, however, are required to complete that formulation. It must be added that the psychological states constitute causes of the action *relative to that person*, when the qualification conveys both (1) that in another person at that time this may not be so, and (2) that for the same person at another time (i.e. later or earlier in his or her life) this may not hold. The unique psychological makeup of any individual personality means that, while A might not have done X because she was deranged, B might have done so although sane. Similarly, the possibility of extensive personality change through time means that, while at t_1 A would not have done X unless he was deranged, at t_2 he might have done so while sane.

The widespread acceptance of these attitudes concerning madness and moral responsibility was associated with the appearance of a secular and medical understanding of madness which gained significance with the decline of an earlier, religious one.

In the medieval period, demonic possession was believed to cause madness: depriving people of their reason, according to the fifteenth-century *Malleus Malificarum* (Sprenger and Kraemer, 1486) was Lucifer's sixth way of injuring humanity. On into the seventeenth century, moreover, the insane were accused as witches and sorcerers (Walker, 1982), typical treatment of whom is illustrated in the following account of a man in Königsburg in 1636, who would today be judged psychotic (cited by Zilboorg and Henry, 1941, p. 259):

> [he] thought he was God the Father; he claimed that all the angels and the devil and the Son of God recognized his power. He was convicted. His tongue was cut out, his head cut off, and his body burned

It was only with the emergence of a medical conception of madness that there came a lifting of moral blame. By the eighteenth century, as one authority places it (Zilboorg and Henry, 1941, p. 280),

> Mental disease was finally wrested [by medicine] from the clutches of superstitious sadism [and] began to be looked upon as the misfortunes of man

At last the insane came to be viewed as 'ill' or 'sick' people, whose miserable state, as Pinel puts it, 'deserves all the consideration due to suffering humanity'.

This view of madness as an unwelcome visitation for which blame would be inappropriate emerged slowly, alongside a gradual emphasis on the notion of madness as akin to other physical ailments receiving medical treatment, and it is naturally suggested by the medical picture. Our attitudes towards the physically sick are expressed in the language of passivity in which a person is said to *suffer* a disease, and it happens despite his or her every wish and intention.

The medical view of madness is germane to the belief that the insane are blameless in having their condition (*Belief 1*).

Moreover, the adoption of a medical point of view was historically a central ingredient in its emergence – although it need not be assumed that the one directly caused the other, since each may have separately reflected the secular spirit of the time. Either way, with the medical understanding of madness came vast humanitarian advances of the utmost significance in the history of madness. Acknowledging this historical connection and debt, however, does not require that a medical understanding be seen as the only one able to accommodate the belief that madness is not blameworthy, as I shall argue later. It is important that the undeniable historical link between the two not be confused with any closer conceptual tie.

And now let us consider the parallel but separate stance concerning madness and moral responsibility which casts madness as an excuse for action (*Belief 2*). This position is reflected in the legal use of insanity as a defence, whereby the insane wrongdoer is not held to have been responsible, or fully so, for his or her action, nor to be rightly subject to ordinary blame and punishment for it. Insanity functions here as do other grounds for excuse, whose presence – at least in the case of crimes carrying severe penalties – renders the accused less than fully liable: mistake, accident, provocation and duress.

There were attempts to formulate the moral principle which provided the basis of the modern insanity plea by the sixteenth century. It is clear, for example, in the following excerpt from a handbook written for English Justices of the Peace and dated 1581 (to be discussed fully in a later chapter), where the insane are exempted from blame for actions taken without an 'understanding wil' (Lambard, 1581),

> If a mad man or a natural foole, or a lunatike in the time of his lunacie, or a childe y apparently hath no knowledge of good nor evil do kil a ma, this is no felonious act, nor any thing forfeited by it . . . for they cannot be said to have any understanding wil. But if upon examinatio it fal out y they knew what they did, & y it was ill, the seemeth it to be otherwise

Again, we find it expressed by the eighteenth century jurist, Blackstone (1765–7, p. 433). Speaking of a want or defect of the will which excuses from the guilt of crimes, he includes the 'deficiency of will' which arises,

> . . . from a defective or vitiated understanding, vis., in an idiot or a lunatic

and goes on

> for the rule of law as to the latter . . . is that 'furios furore solum punitar'. In criminal cases, therefore, idiots and lunatics are not chargeable for their own acts, if committed when under these incapacities: not even for treason itself

Before the end of the nineteenth century this principle had been formally laid down along with rules for determining the presence of exculpating insanity. Later, police and judicial authorities were accorded the extensive powers they enjoy today for the diversion of seemingly insane suspects to civil rather than criminal commitment procedures (see Goldstein, 1967).

As my previous remarks on culpability and control suggest, these attitudes or beliefs about the relationship between madness and moral responsibility will depend on how we regard madness in other respects. Were it possible regularly to predict and prevent the onset of madness, then we should be inclined to relinquish them.

Yet it is also true that, for those by whom these beliefs are accepted, the understanding or framework we adopt of madness will be expected to take them into account, to be compatible with them and even to explain and justify them. In this book I shall show that the medical understanding or 'model' of madness, which has been associated with the emergence of these beliefs and is defended on account of its supposed accommodation of them, fails to meet this test. Contrary to what has usually been accepted, I shall argue that if we adopt such beliefs about madness and responsibility we must look for an alternative account to the medical one.

Notes

1 In speaking of 'our' conviction here and throughout the book, I refer to the group of those – including myself – who are moved to treat insanity as exculpating. This impulse is not universal, and I acknowledge that there is disagreement over particular cases even among those sharing it. (This disagreement is discussed in Chapter 11).
2 My stipulation concurs, for example, with the recent statement by the American Psychiatric Association (1982, p. 11) that

any revision of the insanity defense standards should indicate that mental disorders potentially leading to exculpation must be *serious*. Such disorders should usually be of the severity (if not always of the quality) of conditions that psychiatrists diagnose as *psychoses*

and with the wording of the Bonnie Rule (Bonnie, 1982):

> . . . the terms mental disease or mental retardation include only those severely abnormal mental conditions that grossly and demonstrably impair a person's perception or understanding of reality and that are not attributable primarily to the voluntary ingestion of alcohol or other psychoactive substances.

3 e.g. in the proposal that the insanity plea be abolished in favour of a traditional *mens rea* requirement.
4 Except in special cases, e.g. when – in the case of desires – the impulse is irresistibly strong. The starving man's hunger may represent an excuse for his stealing food, but not – unless he acts compulsively and is drawn by an irresistible force – the hunger of a man who ate breakfast that day.

2

A Disease Model of Madness

In discussions of the history and philosophy of madness it is the practice to describe comprehensive theories offering explanations of that state together with broad paradigms in terms of which it may be understood as *models*. The most commonly distinguished one of these is known as a medical model, which is prevalent and pervasive today despite attacks from the anti-psychiatry movement.

This model depends on perceived analogies between madness and certain aspects of clinical medicine, such as its view of the disease process, its conception of aetiology, its characteristic practices and procedures and the social attitudes and roles it invites. Thus a medical model has been defined (Bates, 1977, p. 10) as resting on

> . . . a belief that mental illness is a disease process, with an organic or biochemical underlying cause, with certain symptoms, and specific treatments and prognoses

Rather than speaking of one all-encompassing medical model as this quotation does, however, it is more accurate to speak of a variety of medical models. While the formulation quoted reflects the most thoroughgoing application of the analogy between madness and physical ill health, any one of several aspects of clinical medicine would be sufficient for establishing it; there are, in psychiatry, systems or 'models' which incorporate some but not all aspects described – most notably, perhaps, psychoanalysis which adopts the practices and terminology, without most of the theoretical tenets, of a medical point of view. The above quotation describes a model of madness which, to avoid confusion, I shall refer to as the disease model. The disease model derives its force from medical theories as to the nature of disease. Because it reflects the most thoroughgoing appeal to a medical point of view,

I shall concentrate my discussion upon this model. What I am about to say, then, will not always hold true for other accounts, like the psychoanalytic one, even though they too may be described as medical models.

The plausibility of this model relies on the central analogy underlying it: that between the psychological states and behaviour comprising what can be observed of madness – its manifestations, as I shall call them – and the symptoms of a physical ailment. As long as this analogy is warranted, then much else follows. Madness has physical causes analogous to the causes of physical diseases. It is appropriately treated in a medical setting. Its sufferers are rightly seen as victims of their condition and as blameless for having it. The terminology of 'therapy', 'cure', 'prognosis', etc., and a system of medical nosology, rightly apply. Thus, on one of its original and most important formulations, the model was defined (Veatch, 1973, p. 93) as that within which deviancy is seen as,

> (a) non-voluntary, and (b) organic, if (c) the class of relevant, technically-competent experts is physicians and if (d) it falls below some socially defined minimal standard of acceptability

The concept of disease is vague and inadequately defined in medical texts. However, a few general observations seem to hold true. In non-psychiatric medicine, diseases are regarded as entities whose characteristic signs and symptoms are their more readily observable effects. Although these symptoms may be psychological states (an intense thirst, for example), it seems to be understood that they result from known or ultimately discoverable underlying states of organic malfunction. [The exact definition of this alteration or malfunction raises complex issues, as has been shown (Margolis, 1976). For our purposes here, however, it is sufficient to acknowledge that the somatic condition is present, and these further complexities may be omitted.] Thus the German authority Virchow (1858) writes, 'there is no general, only local, disease'[1], which may be interpreted to read that disease pertains not to the whole person but to that person's particular anatomical parts.

The relationship between underlying states of disease and their signs and symptoms is revealed in the contrast between the role of the pathologist, who is directly concerned with the disease itself, and that of the clinician, who encounters only its symptoms. Analysing the nature of clinical judgement in medicine, Feinstein (1967, pp. 73–4) cites some typical diagnostic categories (e.g. myocardial infarcation) and comments:

> Not a single one of these diagnostic terms represents an entity which is ever actually seen, heard, or touched in the ordinary bedside observation of a clinician. Every one of these entities is an abnormality of internal anatomical structure. The clinician at the bedside never observes these abnormal structures directly; he observes the symptoms and signs which are their clinical effects . . . the only doctor who regularly witnesses the actual, complete appearance of all these anatomic entities . . . is a pathologist

Not only are the underlying disease states with which the pathologist is concerned separable from their signs and symptoms, the underlying malfunction – either known or presumed – while not sufficient for the ascription of disease seems to be a necessary or *sine qua non* condition of that ascription. There cannot be said to be signs and symptoms in the absence of an underlying disease state.

An epistemological explanation of the latter convention is also revealed in the passage quoted: from the presence of signs and symptoms often associated with certain diseases, it is not possible to infer the presence of the underlying malfunction with certainty. Neither the individual symptoms taken alone, nor even a set or syndrome of symptoms, is sufficient always for the presence of the particular disease state to be inferred from them.[2] This point, too, is illustrated by Feinstein (1967, pp. 68–9):

> Anginal pain may arise from pulmonary hypertension, not coronary disease; coronary disease may produce no angina. Skin may look yellow because of hypercarotenemia; a serum bilirubin value may be elevated without evidence of clinical jaundice

Thus, while clinical conditions have often been identified by their symptoms in the absence of any knowledge of their underlying disease state, it is a presumption in medicine that these underlying states of malfunction are present. This presumption seems to be one of the factors distinguishing disease from what is called injury, which may comprise only symptoms, produced by some external cause like a blow on the head (although this is not a distinction which has always been respected, as has been pointed out) (Culver and Gert, 1982).

Because the notion of a disease entity refers to underlying organic states of the person in this way, drawing an analogy between the psychological manifestations or 'symptoms' of madness, on the one hand, and the symptoms of ordinary physical diseases, on the other – as the disease model of madness does – presupposes that the 'disease' of schizophrenia, for example, refers not – or not only – to the psychological states making up its 'symptoms' (hallucinations, thought disorder, etc.), but also to unknown physical states of malfunction producing them.

It is important to stress again here that I describe only one medical model. To begin with there may be other models according to which schizophrenia is conceived as a medical condition, not by virtue of its nature but because of some aspect of the way it is treated. Moreover, madness may be analogized with other conditions: illness, for example, or malady – although I believe that neither the notion of illness nor that of malady yields a useful medical model of madness, even though they each avoid some of the difficulties inherent in the more thoroughgoing disease analogy.[3,4]

Accepting for the present the plausibility of the underlying analogy – which, we shall see, may be questioned – a further issue remains to be clarified. Are mental diseases merely to be treated as *like* physical ones or are they to be treated as physical diseases? Stimulated by the discovery of organic conditions of a psychiatric nature, such as the nineteenth-century realization that general paresis of the insane was the result of syphilitic infection, the analogy has widely been taken to warrant an identification. Marked parallels between the symptoms of general paresis and other brain diseases and injuries – like toxic reactions and senility, on the one hand, and nonorganic or 'functional' disorders like schizophrenia and depression, on the other – suggest the presence of underlying organic malfunction in the latter. Mental disorders are often spoken of as diseases even in the case of functional conditions which want for any widely accepted explanation in organic terms and are as yet identified only as a set of psychological and behavioural manifestations. What was once a metaphorical extension has come to acquire a literal meaning.

In what follows, however, I shall adopt the more cautious convention of referring to the medical model as presupposing an analogy, not an identity, between madness and physical disease. Madness then is a 'disease' – not a disease – in my formulation of the disease model.

The Sick Role

Medical models have been characterized in terms of certain social roles they invited. The so-called sick role played, it is claimed, as well by persons who are mentally 'diseased' or 'sick' as by those who are physically so,[5,6] includes four items, known as Parsons' Postulates after their initial formulation by the sociologist Talcott Parsons (1951):

(i)   the sick person is exempted from some or all of her 'normal social responsibilities' [relative, Parsons adds, to the severity of the illness];
(ii) the sick person is treated as not having been able to help getting ill and not able to get well by an act of decision or will [In this sense, Parsons points out, the sick person is 'exempted from responsibility' and in a condition that must be taken care of.];
(iii) the sick person is expected to want to get well;
(iv) the sick person is treated as expected to seek appropriate, usually medical help and to cooperate with that help towards the end of getting well.

The notion of responsibility appealed to in the first two of these tenets is insufficiently developed in Parsons' work and we cannot be sure of the kind and limits of responsibility he intended. However, (i) and (ii) have been understood to describe exemption from moral responsibility for serious acts of wrongdoing as well as for lesser omissions and failings [e.g. by Osmond and Seigler (1974) whose work will be discussed at some length in the following pages]. Thus they may be taken to reflect attitudes concerning the same kind of blamelessness which, as we saw in the last chapter, is ascribed to the insane – apparently confirming the appropriateness of deeming them 'sick' in the same way as those who are physically afflicted.

Several benefits – practical, procedural and theoretical – are thought by its proponents to distinguish a medical model. One attempt has been made to evaluate systematically other models of madness *vis-à-vis* the medical ones: in a comparison between a medical model and five others (the moral, impaired, psychoanalytic, conspiratorial and family interaction models), Osmond and Seigler (1974, p. 172) conclude:

> At almost every point – even, unexpectedly, with regard to aetiology and treatment – the medical model is at least equal to, and usually has an edge over, all its competitors

Advantages are cited like the medical model's accommodation of mistaken diagnoses, its greater refinement of diagnostic categories providing increased 'scientific potential', as well as advantages in the dimension of treatment (p. 177) in prognosis (p. 180), and so on. In addition, one theoretical advantage to the medical model is emphasized. A medical model like the one I have been describing has been regarded not only as historically responsible for the acknowledgement of the two important moral beliefs concerning madness outlined in the previous chapter, but also as offering an accommodation of those attitudes which will justify our adoption and maintenance of them. One of the primary functions of a medical model, as it has been put, is to remove culpability (Veatch, 1973), and so central has the moral or ethical element of a medical model been seen to be that it has sometimes been entitled an ethico–medical model (Edwards, 1982). The link between the sick role associated with a medical model and the beliefs concerning madness, blamelessness and responsibility introduced in the previous chapter has been used to justify and support the adoption of a medical model in preference to others.

Thus other models, Osmond and Seigler (1974, p. 195) conclude,

> . . . do not meet our need to uphold the morality of society . . . so far only the medical model has shown a capacity for resolving these complicated problems (concerning culpability) . . . (and providing for) a class of people who, although they have committed a criminal act, are nevertheless at the same time entitled to the sick role

and they speak of a medical model's offering 'the advantage of a blame-free interpretation of behaviour' (p. 176).

However, this connection between adopting a medical model and excusing the insane has not gone unquestioned by the anti-psychiatry critique, and it is one which I too shall contest.

The Anti-psychiatry Critique

Bodily causes of madness such as those referred to in the humoral theory, have been proposed since ancient times, but the practice of understanding and treating madness as analogous to physical disease developed and grew with the importance of clinical medicine itself. Some authorities date the full presence of a medical model to the beginning of the last century, but there are many earlier indications of its influence – for example, the story of Teresa of Avila, who made appeal to a disease analogy in the sixteenth century and succeeded, by doing so, in saving a group of nuns from the Inquisition. She suggested that the mass hysteria of the nuns may have been explained by physical causes. The nuns, then, she reasoned, could not be regarded as evil but as *comas enfermas* (as if sick) and requiring medical rather than spiritual ministrations (Bates, 1977).

Medical models prevailed unquestioned through the first half of the present century, further strengthened and enhanced by developments in the use of drugs, psychosurgery and other physical, as distinct from psychological, forms of treatment, which seemed to confirm the accuracy of the causal explanations it invited and the treatment procedures they in turn suggested.

In the same decade in which confidence in and acceptance of the medical approach to madness reached its zenith, the anti-psychiatry reaction appeared. Critics like Thomas Szasz (1961) with his influential work on the 'myth' of mental illness cast doubt on the deepest underpinnings of the disease model – the analogy with physical disease.

The anti-psychiatry critique, both of medical models and of other aspects of traditional psychiatry, has been unremitting since the early writing of Szasz in the USA and of R. D. Laing in the UK. In this chapter I shall discuss certain anti-psychiatry arguments directed at the medical models in particular; (in later chapters I shall address two other anti-psychiatry theses: the view, associated with Laing, that the insane are as rational as the sane and the claim that the increased medical influence on madness has served to alienate the insane). Anti-psychiatry attacks on medical models have encompassed slogans and stances too weak to warrant discussion as well as serious objections, however, so I shall restrict myself to three of its central theoretical criticisms, all of which were marshalled by Szasz.

First, it is asserted that since to classify someone as mad is to introduce a normative judgement while to classify someone as ill or diseased is not, madness cannot rightly be seen as a medical condition. Secondly, the medical model of madness is said to rest on a false analogy, since it is argued that madness is caused socially rather than biologically or chemically. Thirdly, the aspect of the medical model which exempts the insane from culpability for actions taken because of their condition is questioned; it is asserted, instead, that the freedom and dignity of the mad person requires that they be seen as responsible in the ordinary way.

The weakness of the first attack, resting as it does on the implausible notion that physical medicine is itself a non-normative enterprise, has been thoroughly explored and exposed (Dubos, 1971; Sigwick, 1973) and I shall say no more about it.

The second argument requires closer attention. Szasz concludes that there is no such thing as mental illness because the notions of 'illness' or 'disease' imply the presence of some alteration of organic or bodily structure – a requirement, he insists, which is not met in the case of madness; this conception of disease was established and accepted in medicine until it was subverted by a misapplication of medical thinking to early psychiatry. Thus Szasz (1983, pp. 62–4) states that

> Until the middle of the nineteenth century, and beyond, illness meant a bodily disorder whose typical manifestations were an alteration of bodily structure . . .

and

> since in this original meaning of it, illness was identified by altered bodily structures, physicians distinguished diseases from non-diseases according to whether or not they could detect an abnormal change in the structure of a person's body

Modern psychiatry, he goes on,

> . . . began not by identifying such diseases by means of the established methods of pathology, but by creating a new criterion of what constitutes disease; to the established criterion of detectable alteration of *bodily structure* was now added the fresh criterion of alteration of *bodily functions;* and, as the former was detected by observing the patient's body, so the latter was detected by observing his behaviour

The early nineteenth-century psychiatrists E. Kraepelin and E. Bleuler are particularly singled out as being responsible for this change. According to Szasz (1983, p. 92), they subtly redefined 'the criterion of disease from histopathology to psychopathology' and in so doing 'managed to bring about the great epistemological transformation of our medical age'.

Szasz's conclusion is overstated, however, and his arguments are flawed. It is true, as critics have pointed out, that his historical analysis is too simple. Szasz pictures the organic notion of disease as having prevailed uncontested in early medicine and this is not accurate. While it was associated with the school of Aesculapius at the medical academy of Knidos in ancient Greece, there was another competing and contemporary school in Kos, associated with Hippocrates, which emphasized the more human and holistic notion of the patient's complaint (Pies, 1979).

Although Szasz should have acknowledged the holistic emphasis, I shall argue that much of the apparent support for the holistic concept derives from inexact use of terminology and a failure to put each position precisely. If they are carefully stated there need be no serious incompatibility between the organic concept of disease and the more holistic emphasis on human suffering with which it is usually contrasted.

Some of the difficulty here concerns the technical question of access to the underlying malfunction presupposed in an organic notion of disease. Because many diseases are still known and identified by their symptoms rather than by any underlying organic condition, the position at which Szasz seems to hint – that the organic malfunction must be *observable* – is overstated. The organic malfunction must be *presupposed;* it does not have to be observed for the accurate ascription of the term 'disease'.

Moreover, Szasz need not suggest, as he seems to do, that the underlying state is a sufficient condition for the accurate ascription of the term 'disease'. An organic concept of disease requires only that it be a necessary one. Thus the importance of suffering – present, it has been pointed out, in the etymology of 'pathology', which derives from the Greek 'pathos' – need not be denied. Indeed, it has been argued (Margolis, 1976) that the notion of an underlying organic malfunction central to the organic view presupposes reference to the holistic notion of the disease sufferer as a person, since only by appeal to social norms can the idea of organic malfunction be fully explained. An organic view need not preclude the importance of the nonorganic features of disease which are emphasized in a more holistic account.

Unnecessary confusion surrounds this dispute, in addition, because of a failure to respect the nuances between the term 'disease' on the one hand and the broader 'illness' on the other – a failure of which Szasz himself is guilty. The organic view at least as it is expressed in the work of Virchow, and as I would use it, concerns the application of the term 'disease' – not that of 'illness'. This linguistic distinction has been discussed and developed in the literature where it is claimed, for example, that we reserve ascriptions of illness to human rather than to animal suffering (Boorse, 1975) and illness is defined as a 'diseased state manifest to the agent through that agent's symptoms' (Margolis, 1976). Szasz's efforts to state and defend the organic view, as well as attempts to attack it, are both hampered by a conflation of the two notions of disease and illness. And failure to acknowledge the nuances distinguishing disease and illness has led to an exaggeration of the incompatibility between the organic and holistic positions.

In conclusion, then, while Szasz gives an inadequate account of this position, it seems plausible to adopt the Virchowian view of disease whereby the term is not rightly applied unless with a presumption of the presence of an underlying organic defect of some kind. Szasz seems to suppose that this invalidates the claim of the defenders of a disease model of madness; it does not, but it commits them to the thesis that there is an organic substructure to the observable psychological and behavioural manifestations of madness.

Finally, anti-psychiatry has addressed that aspect of a medical model which concerns culpability: the view that the mad person is rightly exempted from blame and punishment because of his or her condition. The anti-psychiatry attack, in this case, involves a rejection of the underlying moral intuitions. It is argued that providing excuses for the deranged is incompatible with an acknowledgement of the freedom and human dignity which is their due. Szasz, for example, rejects the insanity plea which embodies these intuitions and argues for the restitution of the insane sufferer's right to censure, blame and – in the legal sphere – normal trial.

I do not accept this last position; instead, I wish to endorse the moral intuitions underlying the sick role. Nevertheless, my main criticism of the medical models focuses on this issue of responsibility. In contrast both to the view adopted by Szasz, and anti-psychiatry, and to that attributed to the disease (or ethico-medical) model, it will be argued here that, while the insane should be exempted from blame and punishment, appeal to a medical model will not entirely justify adopting this stance towards them. The attitudes can, and ought to be, adopted but not because of any analogy between madness and physical disease. Thus I differ from Szasz on this issue both on moral and on theoretical grounds. My conclusion concerning the morality of withholding blame from the insane is opposed to Szasz's, and so also is my assessment of the relationship between that moral stance and medical models.

In order to state precisely the position I wish to put forward with regard to the inadequacy of medical models *vis-à-vis* the moral beliefs about madness isolated and refined in Chapter 1, it is important to distinguish them again. *Belief 1* (Madness is not blameworthy) asserts that the mad person is blameless in having his or her condition; *Belief 2* (Madness mitigates blame for wrongdoing) asserts the blamelessness concerning actions undertaken because of that condition. My critique of medical models is related to each separate belief. Of the first I want to point out that a disease model is not, as Osmond and Seigler and its other supporters generally seem to have supposed, unique in accommodating it. An analysis of madness conceived as a certain want of reason, for example, can do so equally well. When a want of reason is seen as something for which its sufferers are not responsible we may – and do – regard them as blameless victims of their condition. This is confirmed by the way blame is withheld from children because of their want of reason or pre-rationality.

Children are as much victims of their age as the sick are of their bodily condition and its causes, and it is generally supposed that children are not – or should not be – blamed for their want of judgement or errors of action stemming from it.

Moreover, the belief is conveyed without the help of the disease analogy in common references to forms of derangement as emotional disorders. The term 'emotional' here, I would suggest, signals not so much that the sufferer's emotions are disordered (the expression is used as much for those with cognitive as for those with primarily emotional disturbances), but that something importantly akin to the emotions happen to him or her – that the language of passivity is appropriate.

Let us also consider those qualifications on *Belief 1* related to the role played by further knowledge of their condition, which would put the power of prevention and control in mad people's hands. The physically sick are not today themselves always entirely innocent victims. A necessary condition of the belief is one which until recently in the history of medicine could be relied upon. Knowledge of the causes and thus the power of prevention, with many serious medical conditions, lay beyond the reach of the sufferer. Indeed, today it eludes sufferer and clinician alike in many cases: for example, the cause and cure of multiple sclerosis are both unknown. Yet today, with widespread education and advances in medicine, it is also true that the requisite power of prevention has been delivered to the sufferers of some conditions, and with this power has come a weakening of the belief in their total innocence. A person whose lung cancer comes from a habit voluntarily and knowingly undertaken and maintained – smoking – is not quite the blameless victim, in our eyes, that the multiple sclerosis sufferer is. This is because of ignorance of the latter condition. With more advances in medicine, we may suppose, the 'victims' of physical disease will come to be less and less the victims we today deem them to be. The traditional conception of a medical model, resting as it is seen to do on the patient's nonculpability, will have to be revised.

We must doubt the claim that only a medical model will accommodate the first belief about madness and moral responsibility (*Belief 1:* Madness is not blameworthy). More important and far-reaching, however, is my criticism of the second attitude (*Belief 2:* Madness mitigates blame for wrongdoing). The strength of a medical model, we have seen, is thought to lie not in its historical link with the emergence of social attitudes expressing this view of the nonculpability of the insane, but in its providing a warrant or justification for that intuition. It is usually proposed as a model which both spawned and adequately accommodates the view. While I do not question the historical connection between medicine and the attitude, I shall cast doubt on the notion that all medical models can accommodate and justify it. Construing madness as if it were a disease, I shall argue in Chapter 3, will not adequately explain why it functions to excuse.

Notes

1 'Es gibt Keine Allgemein Krankheiten, es gibt nur Local Krankheiten.'
2 Wittgenstein's discussion of symptoms and criteria provides an epistemological analysis of the distinction drawn here between underlying causes and symptoms.
3 Additional support for the organic concept of disease outlined here is to be found in ordinary language as Moore has shown (Moore, 1980, p. 48): we speak more naturally of a person as having (in the sense of possessing) a disease rather than being diseased and bodies or some part(s) of them, rather than persons, are the normal subject of the predicate 'diseased'.
4 However, separate problems arise when madness is analogized with other conditions: illness, for example. As the holistic connotation of the notion of illness suggests, being ill apparently entails having a complaint – something wrong or painful of which one is aware. Yet those afflicted by several serious forms of madness may be both oblivious to their condition and in no way pained or (subjectively) disadvantaged by it. Moore (1980, p. 51) has argued that the presence of *impairment*, rather than subjectively acknowledged pain and distress, is at the core of the notion of illness, asserting that a painless paralysis, if capable of improvement, will naturally be described as an illness. Such a paralysis, I would insist, is only an illness because of the subjective awareness – if not of pain, then of the incapacity.
   In a recent attempt to avoid the problems inherent in the disease analogy, Culver and Gert (1982) have proposed that 'malady' be introduced to describe the mental conditions we are concerned with, as well as other physical conditions. A person is defined as suffering a malady 'if and only if he has a condition other than his rational beliefs and desires, such that he is suffering, or at increased risk of suffering an evil (death, pain, disability, loss of freedom or opportunity, or loss of pleasure) in the absence of distinct sustaining cause' (p. 81). But this definition raises problems of its own. Not only does the term have strong ordinary language connotations which go against its use for severe physical conditions (it seems more naturally restricted to lesser ailments, like indigestion). More important, it covers conditions like subjectively defined unattractiveness and baldness about which we are as uncertain over extending the medical model as we are about madness.
5 Those extending this analysis to psychiatric conditions seem to use 'disease', 'sickness' and 'illness' as rough synonyms here, not acknowledging the nuances which distinguish these terms.
6 As well as playing the sick role, it is claimed, the mentally 'sick' attribute Aesculapian authority to the clinicians treating their condition – that authority accorded when, in ordinary physical medicine, patients put themselves in the hands of a physician.

'Aesculapian' authority, on its sociological analysis, comprises three elements: sapiential authority accorded on the basis of the physician's professional knowledge; moral authority derived from the physician's concern with the good of the patient and the morally commendable goal of alleviating suffering; and, finally, charismatic authority which permits the physician some of the special licence extended to priests. These notions have been developed by Osmond and Seigler (1973).

3
Diseases as Excuses for Wrongdoing

The presence of serious physical disease or illness in a person alters our conception of their situation. It engenders sympathy and compassion, and it seems on the face of things to invite a mitigation of ordinary blame and censure when, in everyday situations, that person is guilty of wrongdoing and, particularly, of omission as a result of it. When we learn of a person's flu, we see her absence from the meeting differently. However, I shall argue that a closer look at these impulses towards disease sufferers reveals a rather different picture. Those who are diseased are sometimes excused, it is true, but not exactly on account of their disease and when disease invites us to lessen blame and punishment in a legal context it is as a merciful gesture rather than an act dictated by justice.

We have no inclination to excuse wrongdoers simply because they are diseased; his angina would be irrelevant to our judgement on the rapist's crime. Moreover, when we wish to excuse a crime which was caused by a disease – as a brain tumour sufferer's might be said to be – it is, as I shall now show, because we appeal to one of the traditional excusing conditions of ignorance and compulsion and not because of the role played by the disease as such. And while feelings of sympathy for the sick sometimes encourage us to act mercifully towards them by withholding the blame which is their due, mercy and justice are different motives and must not be confused.

I shall look at why diseases as such do not serve to excuse wrongdoing and then examine the role of merciful gestures in this context, but first the notion of excuses must be considered.

Excuses

We assert that an agent had an excuse in order to lessen blame or culpability for harm done, or when we are said to have done something which is, as Austin puts it in his important 'A Plea for

Excuses' to which I referred earlier, 'bad, wrong, inept, unwelcome, or in some other of the numerous possible ways untoward'
(Austin, 1956–7, p. 176). Excuse, then is distinguished from
justification: when we offer an excuse, we admit the conduct was
bad but do not accept responsibility; while offering justification
we accept responsibility but deny that the conduct was bad
(Austin 1956–7).

Three kinds of harmful deeds and omissions have traditionally
been regarded as exempt from full culpability both in moral and
legal thinking: (1) involuntary movements of the body or omissions due to physical incapacities (I am jostled so that I push you
into a puddle, or my rheumatism keeps me bedridden so that I
cannot attend the funeral); (2) action or omission which is
compelled (under threats to my life I sign a fraudulent document,
or knowing that to do so would worsen my bronchitis so as to
seriously endanger my health I do not finish by a publisher's
deadline); and finally (3) action or omission from nonculpable
ignorance (trying to help I administer a fatal dose of medicine
which has been wrongly labelled, or out of forgetfulness brought
on by senility I omit to report a crime). Of these only (2) and (3)
count, strictly, as actions. The first is merely a movement of my
body, not an action. We offer excuses for actions only: movements or omissions due to physical inabilities are done involuntarily; they explain and exculpate but they do not excuse. We find
a theory of this sort in Aristotle's account of responsibility:
'Those things are thought involuntary, which take place under
compulsion or owing to ignorance' (*Nichomachean Ethics* 110a).

Both (2) and (3) require qualification. Psychological compulsion has often been equated with action or omission which is
compelled like that described in (2) above. While this equation
must be questioned, as we shall see, I would add certain compulsive and phobic behaviour as a subset of (2) and a fourth group of
deeds and omissions rightly regarded as exempt from full culpability. Since much culpable action involves some ignorance, let us
qualify (3) by adding that people act from ignorance when they do
not know what they do, some of the more obvious consequences
of their act (both examples offered above fit this category) or why
they do it. Aristotle says '[It is on] ignorance of particulars i.e. of
the circumstances of the action and the objects with which it is
concerned . . . that both pity and pardon depend' (*Nichomachean
Ethics* 111a).

Acts of wrongdoing caused by disease are often excusable, as some of the above examples illustrate (I fail to meet the deadline due to the bronchitis, or out of senile forgetfulness I do not report the crime). They are not excusable in these cases, however, because they result from disease. Rather, as I shall show, the presence of one or the other of the traditional excusing conditions of ignorance and compulsion explains our impulse to excuse.

The Disease Analogy

The analogy with physical disease on the basis of which madness is conceived as a medical condition invites a series of false and misleading beliefs. The first of these is that an underlying physical condition (a state of chemical imbalance, for example, or a brain lesion), rather than the person's beliefs and desires, counts as the cause of any act of wrongdoing it might occasion. If this were true, then another belief would follow: that when a person acts because of such a physical condition, that person acts *involuntarily*. If both these beliefs were correct, then the defender of a medical model of madness could rightly conclude that when there is a disease there is an excuse for wrongdoing. Both beliefs and conclusion, however, are mistaken.

The confused line of reasoning outlined here seems still to underlie much contemporary thinking about mental disease, although it is not always explicitly stated. We find it in a US Supreme Court reference to a disease analysis of alcoholism, for example (Minority opinion, p. 561, *Powell* v. *Texas*). Regarded as a disease, alcoholism must be seen as

> caused and maintained by something other than the moral fault of the alcoholic, something that, to a greater or lesser extent depending on the physiological or psychological makeup and history of the individual, *cannot be controlled by him* [my emphasis]

A more detailed discussion is seen in the findings of the New Hampshire Supreme Court, which anticipated the starkly medical thinking of the Durham decision by nearly one hundred years. Influenced by the writing of Isaac Ray whose important *Treatise on the Medical Jurisprudence of Insanity* (1838) put forward an analysis of madness as brain disease, the court's Justice Doe proposed that being an 'offspring or product of mental disease' should be the criterion for criminal insanity. Thus he argued (*State* v. *Pike*, p. 441):

> For if the alleged act of a defendant was the act of his mental disease it was not in law his act, and he is no more responsible for it than he would be if it had been the act of his involuntary intoxication or of another person using the defendant's hand against his utmost resistance . . . when a disease is the propelling, uncontrollable power, the man is innocent as the weapon – the mental and moral elements are as guiltless as the material. If his mental, moral and bodily strength is subjugated and pressed to an involuntary service, it is immaterial whether it is done by disease or by another man or a brute or any physical force or art or nature set in operation without any fault on his part

The analogy Doe draws with a person using the defendant's hand against his utmost resistance is telling. Were the defendant's hand thus propelled, the resultant alleged action of the defendant would not be regarded as *his* action – indeed we would not regard it as an action, strictly, at all but as a movement. Moreover, it would be seen as *involuntary* and the defendant judged nonculpable.

However, the analogy is false. Consider the case of a schizophrenic who commits homicide because of his (false) belief that he does God's will. We may allow, with Doe, that underlying this man's schizophrenic psychological condition are organic states of dysfunction, but still there are significant disanalogies between this case and that of the defendant who is forced to move his hand. Madness affects psychological states: beliefs and desires enter into the explanation of the schizophrenic's deed in a way they do not that of the defendant forced to move his hand. Even if, in some sense, the beliefs and desires could be said to 'cause' the schizophrenic to act, it can hardly be in the same way as that in which a person is physically forced to move. Physical diseases do sometimes determine our movement or lack thereof, as when a paralysis precludes action (I am unable to move my car when it is illegally parked), but when they affect action mental 'diseases' do so through the mediation of psychological states: what follows are actions, not involuntary movements. (This is not to say, of course, that full moral responsibility will be ascribed to them. We withhold ascriptions of moral responsibility to some of the sane person's actions too, on the grounds that they were done under duress, or out of nonculpable ignorance).

The misapprehensions identified here are invited by the disease analogy. We speak of a physical disease as comprising both underlying causes and symptoms, e.g. the lung infection (underlying cause) and fever (symptom) of tuberculosis. Here it is appropriate to argue that the sufferer is not responsible for his or her fever, not merely because having the fever is part of what we mean by having that disease but, more importantly, because the fever, like the lung infection, is something which happens to us and is beyond our power. Most physical diseases allow this reasoning,[1] but mental 'diseases' do not. Even if the term disease covers both the hypothesized underlying brain state and the psychological and behavioural 'symptoms' of schizophrenia, still from the fact that we are not responsible for the brain state it does not immediately follow that we are not responsible for the 'symptoms'.

The underlying error of reasoning which encourages this false analogy is summed up in another early New Hampshire case. No argument is needed, it states (*State* v. *Jones*, p. 394),

> to show that to hold that a man may be punished for what is the offspring of disease would be to hold that a man may be punished for a disease. Any rule which makes that possible cannot be law

Here it is suggested that to be excused from blame for a disease *entails* being excused from blame for actions stemming from that condition.

The mistake in this reasoning was already identified in Chapter 1 where it was explained why the moral beliefs about the blamelessness associated with insanity are two separate ones unconnected by entailment. *Belief 1* (Madness is not blameworthy) was there distinguished from *Belief 2* (Madness mitigates blame for wrongdoing). Just as we might blame people for their violent actions but not for the rage which initiated them, it was there argued, or we might blame them for their greedy actions but not for their appetite, so we must distinguish between holding a person responsible for his or her state of derangement and holding that person responsible for his or her crime.

It follows then that both assumptions outlined earlier in this chapter are false. It is true neither that an underlying physical condition always counts as sufficient for the act of wrongdoing it is said to cause nor that, when a person does something due to such a condition, what that person does is involuntary. From the disease having been produced in us rather than being something we voluntarily embraced, it cannot be assumed that diseases are excuses for the actions they occasion. Diseases *may* prove to constitute excuses for the actions they bring about, but they have not as yet been shown to do so. However, I shall now show that – even when the two questions distinguished above are prized apart and we examine the validity of the separate claim that diseases constitute excuses – we shall find insufficient support to maintain it.

Organic Disorders

Among the ordinary physical diseases which standardly affect action there are a group deserving particular attention: the so-called organic disorders of psychiatry. Organic disorders are those conditions whose physical cause (some kind of structural impairment) is known to medicine – brain tumour, head injuries, toxic reactions and 'brain diseases' such as the arteriosclerotic cerebral degeneration known as senility.

The psychological symptoms of these disorders include hallucination, delusions, 'thought disorder', memory and cognitive failures, and personality change. There is then a strong similarity between the psychological effects of these conditions and of those marking the so-called *functional* disorders, such as schizophrenia, with which the organic disorders are contrasted, whose aetiology remains unknown. Because of the similarity, when such organic disorders cannot be shown to excuse the actions they cause, then there seem to be no grounds for supposing that the functional disorders – constituting what we ordinarily know as insanity – do so.

Before turning to a closer examination of the way organic disorders affect action, it is necessary to stress the force by saying that diseases do not excuse wrongdoing *as such*. Because of the presence of ignorance or compulsion in much action brought about by organic disorders, it is insufficient to discover cases like those described in which our intuitions would encourage us to exonerate the wrongdoers suffering from such conditions. The blamelessness of the disease sufferer may be due to the presence of one or the other of those factors (ignorance or compulsion) and not at all to the action's having been the product of a disease.

Thus, in order to establish whether diseases as such serve to excuse, we must find or artificially fabricate cases where wrong-doing but *neither ignorance nor compulsion* results from an organic condition.

One familiar case actually seems to invite such a description – senility.[2] The presenile and senile dementias take years, some-times even decades, to change substantially the psychology and behaviour of the sufferer and are described as causing slow personality change. Conditions such as these are classified as chronic as distinct from acute forms of cerebral incompetence, and the contrast between descriptions of such chronic conditions and the acute ones (like head injury and toxic reactions) which have rapid onset and course suggests that two different accounts of the relationship between organic condition and resultant crimi-nal action might be distinguished. One is where the action is affected directly, or relatively directly, by the condition and the other is where it is so affected more indirectly:

(1)   *'Direct Effect'* cases where the disease or condition directly results in the particular motive or desire (e.g. a hostile impulse) occasioning the criminal action.

(2)   *'Indirect Effect'* cases where the disease or condition is responsible for a pervasive personality change, and as a result of that change, which rearranges and affects attitudes, beliefs, emotions and sometimes even memories, the crimi-nal action is taken.

In what follows I am going to argue that while we would wish to excuse criminal actions fitting the account given in (1) (*Direct Effect*), descriptions of such cases can never be freed from the elements of ignorance and compulsion. Conversely, although we can exclude the presence of ignorance and compulsion from a description of criminal action fitting the account given in (2) (*Indirect Effect*), we would not be inclined to regard the action as *excusable* in such a case.

One class of cases fitting the description given in (1) (*Direct Effect*) seems to call for further comment: toxic reactions. We usually think of drug-induced criminal action as something the agent ought to have been able to predict and prevent and thus not excusable. In legal contexts, for example, far from drunkenness constituting an *excuse* for illegal actions that it occasions, sometimes it is treated as a distinct crime: thus the double charge of manslaughter and drunken driving.

Where the criminal action resulted from toxic reactions not knowingly or voluntarily induced, however (when, for example, a person is coerced into taking some drug or is justifiably unaware of toxic effects of one taken for legitimate medical purposes), it would seem that the presence of the physical state should and would be taken to constitute an excuse. So the physical condition's having been responsible for the action would not *alone* count as sufficient for our excusing it. In addition, the physical state must itself have been involuntarily or unknowingly induced.

Before examining particular examples illustrating the relationship between physical condition and criminal action, I will specify again what is required.

(a) '*Freedom Requirement*' The criminal action described must not have been undertaken under compulsion or compulsively.
(b) '*Knowledge Requirement*' It must not have been done in ignorance (of what was done and why).
(c) '*Causal Requirement*' It must have been the causal product or effect of the physical condition in the way specified earlier.

If we consider the above requirements in relation to the account of the connection between physical condition and criminal action given in (1) (*Direct Effect*), we may build an example from an actual case.

Sniper Case. In 1966 a sniper on the tower at the University of Texas killed several people and terrorized the community before being shot fatally by police marksmen. A brain tumour revealed at a subsequent autopsy was regarded as having caused the man's actions. Some evidence as to the state of his mind was provided by a note, found subsequently, in which he described experiencing 'mental turmoil' and 'overwhelming violent impulses' which perhaps suggest the presence of an element of compulsion (Sarason and Sarason, 1980). However, we may disregard this reconstruction. On the face of things it seems possible (though perhaps unlikely) that the sniper was neither unaware of what he was doing on the tower, nor compelled to act as he did.

Here an analogous case suggests itself, where again a certain condition occasions an action while the actor apparently acts voluntarily.

Housebreaker Case. A housebreaker acting under the influence of post-hypnotic suggestion may believe that she acts without compulsion and ignorance. Two alternative versions of this case may be distinguished; both seem possible.

(1)   She believes that she acts on an impulse *without* further reasons.
(2)   She has 'rationalized' the action with reasons falsely believed to have occasioned it.

Notice that either of (1) or (2) might be added to our reconstruction of the sniper's state of mind, also. He might have believed himself to act upon an elaborate set of 'reasons', actually 'rationalizations' to explain his action; or he might simply have believed himself to act without reasons, on an impulse.

I believe that we should wish to *excuse* both the sniper and a previously, and involuntarily, hypnotized house breaker. Yet in neither description is the knowledge requirement (b), that the act be performed without ignorance, actually fulfilled. Our law breakers may believe that they act without ignorance, either because they are aware of what they (falsely) take to be the reasons for their action, or because they know none and believe there to be none; moreover, they do know much of the nature and consequences of their deed. They do not act without ignorance, for all that, for they do not know why they act. In the same way, it would seem, it will be difficult to describe any case fitting the account of the relationship between physical condition and criminal action given in (1) (*Direct Effect*) where the disease or condition directly results in the impulse occasioning the criminal action, without failing to fulfil (b). Difficult, yes – but impossible?

In answer the two alternative accounts of the hypnotized housebreaker's mental state, (i) impulse and (ii) 'rationalization' must be examined separately. If we are describing a person's 'rationalizing' her action, believing falsely that some reason motivated it, then it seems correct to say that it will be impossible to fulfil (b) (knowledge requirement). To believe a false explanation of one's action is to be ignorant of one important aspect of one's act: why it was done.

However, the case of what I have called impulse, is different. It seems possible to give an alternative reconstruction of the sniper's state of mind, for example, if we allow that he might have been acting on an impulse such that he was aware *both* of his hostile murderous impulse, and of the presence of his brain tumour and its likely role in occasioning that impulse. In this reconstruction no ignorance of the kind we have been discussing remains; there is knowledge both of the isolated impulse to kill and of its origin.

Yet we are now obliged to reject the example on other grounds. We are describing a person, it will be remembered, who would not have taken such an action had the pathological condition not been present. If so, given the second reconstruction where he entertained an unreasoned impulse to do the criminal action and nothing more, then it seems true to say that the sniper, assuming him to have been of normal moral constitution, would have refrained from acting upon his criminal impulses *unless* that impulse were itself so strong as to be irresistible. For unless a murderous impulse is irresistible it seems that, in the absence of any reason for doing so other than the simple desire itself, it will not be acted upon – except by the truly vicious person who may be capable of killing on impulse but whom we have no inclination to excuse and who is thus not the subject of the present example.

The latter I regard as expressing a common and warranted presumption. It seems that if an otherwise sane person of normal moral constitution commits murder or any other crime of such magnitude on an apparently unreasoned impulse we *assume* either that there was a reason, deeply unconscious perhaps, of which he or she was unaware or that the action was in some way subject to compulsion. Had the impulse not been irresistibly strong then there would not have been a resultant criminal action; had the impulse been irresistible, the description fails (a) (freedom requirement), for an impulse so strong compels us to act and is not voluntary in the way there specified.

There has been shown to be difficulty in imagining a case of the kind characterized in (1) (*Direct Effect*) where the disease or condition directly results in the particular motive or impulse occasioning the criminal action – without failing to fulfil one or both of (a) (freedom requirement) or (b) (knowledge requirement). Descriptions of such cases seem inextricably bound to the elements of ignorance and compulsion: it will always seem that we excuse because of ignorance or compulsion – not disease.

Now we must turn to the second account of the relationship between physical condition and criminal action: (2) (*Indirect Effect*) which allows a gradual personality change intervening between the initial condition and the subsequent criminal action. The notion of personality change requires elucidation. If a person's emotional reactions and actions were to undergo a change so that his or her customary affability, for example, were replaced by suspicion and aloofness, then *in the absence of any change in his or her beliefs and other attitudes or moods* we should hesitate to describe that person as having undergone a personality or character change. I take this to be due to such a change involving a certain pervasiveness and coherence. It affects not only fleeting reactions but also associated and more enduring states, attitudes, beliefs and dispositions. As a corollary of that, true personality or character change in the natural order of things, i.e. excluding brain transplants and other science-fiction practices, could not occur instantaneously. It is necessarily a process which occurs over a period of time. (The significance of these characteristics of personality change will emerge.)

It does seem plausible to describe the criminal actions of sufferers from some slowly developing degenerative disease as done voluntarily and knowingly in the ways specified, while yet as being the result of that condition. The personality traits commonly described as resulting from degenerative brain diseases, suspicion and hostility would seem quite apposite as triggers to wrongdoing. While such a description fits the requirements set out in (a)–(c), the question now becomes one of whether we should be inclined to regard the action as excusable. We are no longer sure, it seems to me, that an excuse is warranted.

If someone suffered a slow but radical alteration of personality as the result of degenerative disease – changing over a matter of years from being passive, gentle and trusting to being aggressive, suspicious and violent, when such characteristics formed part of a whole including attitudes and beliefs as well as more fleeting states – we should hesitate to excuse that person for her criminal action (assuming knowledge and the absence of compulsion), although both we and she understood the role played by the disease in her action.

This intuition, it would seem, rests on a defensible principle. There is a good reason why we should be reluctant to excuse the criminal action of a person suffering long-term personality change. It is because the element of knowledge would appear to enter critically into this case as it did in the case of toxic reactions discussed earlier. Because with knowledge comes foresight and predictive and preventive powers, persons able to understand the disease's role in their motivation and action would be culpable in the same way as the alcoholic or drug addict. They could predict and thus would be held responsible for preventing the illegal actions by avoiding the occasion and means of criminality, or by actively seeking treatment and alleviation for that symptom of their condition. ('Knowledge' here must include an awareness of the symptoms likely to ensue as well as the knowledge that the disease is present.)

(It ought again to be emphasized that, for the purposes of the analysis, we are dealing with artificial or at least highly improbable cases. Knowledge of the presence of the disease and its effects is absent in many cases, sometimes tragically, on the part both of the sufferer and his or her family.)

In addition, a further explanation may be suggested for our reluctance to excuse the disease sufferer whose personality change accounts for his or her criminal action. Part of what makes us pity and exonerate the criminal suffering from an abrupt behaviour change resulting from an acute condition is that we know the condition and its effects to be in every way an unwished-for and repugnant visitation.

However, the case of the sufferer from disease-induced personality change is more complex. Because of the characteristic pervasiveness of such a change, where a number of beliefs and enduring dispositions are involved, it is less easy to assert that the changes brought about and the actions attributable to those changes would be undesirable to the agent. The *changed* person might welcome them: e.g. if her disease changes her over the years from gentle, placid and meek to aggressive and self righteous then she will not wish to have remained – as she would see it – mouselike, cowed and apathetic. We may then look at what the person would have wanted previous to the time of onset of the condition, even if in doing so we are forced to reconstruct a personality long since lost to us. However, in doing so we seem to face another problem: all personalities change over time. There are explanations for personality change more healthy and more common than brain degeneration: experiences themselves, the introduction of new ideas, and so on. Because of the complexity of the process of personality change and the necessary time such change takes, the personality change of someone suffering from a gradually developing degenerative disease is such that we might naturally lose confidence that some other set of conditions may not have occasioned the change in a more healthy and welcome way, if the disease had not.

In this sort of case then it seems impossible to say that the person either finds or would have found the change and resultant action undesirable, as it is possible to say in the cases of action due to acute conditions. In the absence of that parallel it would seem appropriate to equate the cases of long-term personality change with those of ordinary criminal behaviour – as culpable in the ordinary way.

In conclusion then, even if it were possible to show insanity to be a mental disease – rightly so called – we would still have no grounds for supposing that it constituted, *qua* disease, an excuse for the actions of the wrongdoer suffering from it.

Justice and Mercy

Some of the mistaken notion that diseases as such constitute excuses for wrongdoing stems, I think, from a confusion of justice with mercy. As well as stimulating in us a moral intuition to excuse, the sick and suffering engender (other) attitudes of sympathy and compassion. Because of these reactions we are inclined to act mercifully towards them.

The notion of a merciful gesture finds its place beside gestures of forgiveness and grace: what is offered, in each case, is a good which is not understood as a desert. The merciful gesture then, like the forgiving or gracious one, is not obligatory; the quality of mercy is not 'strained'.

The exercise of mercy is illustrated (though not defined) as (Smart, 1968, p. 345):

acknowledging an offense committed, deciding on a just

punishment, and then deciding to exact a punishment of lesser severity than the appropriate or just one

Mercy and justice stem from different sources, as this formulation suggests. When we act mercifully we often give more than what is owed; when we act justly we are required to weigh and distribute exactly what is owed, and no more nor less.

However, it is not always the amount of the gift but rather the nature of the giving which marks the difference between a merciful gesture and a just act and to treat mercy as giving more than what is owed, in the distributive sense, as the formulation quoted above seems to do, is to obscure that point. To act from mercy is not so much to give more than what would be just deserts as to disregard the very notion of desert underlying the concept of justice.

Consider the different ways in which mercy and justice might influence what is, distributively speaking, the same judgment, in a case from criminal justice like the one quoted. A sane criminal is terminally ill. On learning of his condition, we may be moved to alter the sentence we would otherwise have determined as his due – by shortening his jail term, let us say. His plight may elicit compassion, on the one hand, and mercy might dictate that course; on the other hand, we might see the same course as indicated by considerations of justice. However, the decision to lessen the sentence would be reached differently in each case. Whether the wrongdoer knew of his condition when he committed the act of wrongdoing would be insignificant to our response when we act in this way out of mercy. And our indifference to that detail confirms that it is mercy rather than justice from which our impulse springs.

If, on the other hand, we were influenced by considerations of justice, and partially *excused* the man for the wrongdoing, his state of knowledge about his condition would be of critical importance. We might want to say, for example, that concern over his illness and his knowledge of the prognosis had interfered with his rational grasp – had made him desperate, perhaps, or cruel. To argue this, however, would be to offer an excuse which, in ignorance of his plight, the man would not have.

In contrast, mercy eludes the notion of desert. To act out of mercy is precisely to act without consideration of what is owed, given the particular circumstances. It may be said, on some grander scale, that suffering and deprivation are being addressed in the merciful gesture and that to heap further deprivation when the man is soon to be deprived of his life is excessive punishment. It has been suggested, indeed, that there may be 'undefined limits . . . that we cannot refuse to alleviate, or allow anyone to incur, without shame' (Card, 1972, p. 205). But this calculation transcends the modest equation balanced in the scales of justice. God, after all, is described as merciful; humans, more often, strive merely to be just.

Understanding madness as a disease may engender mercy in our response to the criminal sufferer of that condition. It may indeed result in the same mitigation which treating madness as an excuse would do. However, lessening the force of judicial blame out of mercy, which we are free to do, must not be confused with lessening it because considerations of justice so dictate.

The failure of the medical model to accommodate our moral intuition that insanity excuses wrongdoing is a neglected aspect of the standard critiques of that model. It is, moreover, the fundamental failing of a disease model, it seems to me – a more damaging aspect of it than other more familiarly cited defects: its inhumanity, its hidden normativism and its spurious aetiological assumptions. We want to excuse the insane criminal or wrongdoer. Yet if we adopt a medical model we must explain why diseases constitute excuses – and they do not appear to do so.

Notes

1 Not all do so, however. Some diseases have psychological and behavioural symptoms, e.g. a great thirst and the tendency to drink excessively. Here it would be mistaken, as it would in the 'mental disease' case, to conclude that frequent drinking (a symptom) involved involuntary movements.
2 The next section of this chapter is taken directly from Radden (1982).

4

Madness as Unreason

The thesis defended in this book is that, in certain respects, an analysis in terms of what will be called unreason is better suited to an understanding of madness than is the analogy with physical disease which underlies the medical model we have been considering.

The analysis proposed here is one which is grounded in the familiar but neglected equation which allows 'insanity' as a loose equivalent of 'irrationality' and 'sanity' as the equivalent of 'rationality'. It requires that madness be understood as allied to the other illogicalities and irrationalities of sane people in everyday life: of adults, when they are less than fully reasonable, and of children. Clearly there are differences, of kind and degree, between the illogical thought of a sane but muddled person and the thought of a mad one, as there are between that of a child and a mad person. However, what is lost to our understanding of madness by not emphasizing that these cases share a common want of reason far outweighs any gain to be had by distinguishing them.

The term 'unreason' will be introduced as broad enough to capture all the ways in which adults and children show a want of reason. Unlike the expression 'mental disease', this term does not indicate an analogy or model of madness. The kind of madness we are concerned with here is a particular form of nonrationality or unreason.

The unreason analysis of insanity is derived from a time in the history of the understanding of madness in Europe revealed in Michel Foucault's explorations of earlier structures. In the sixteenth and early seventeenth century, if his account is accurate, madness was conceived of primarily as the want of reason its sufferers exhibited and as akin to other, saner manifestations of 'unreason' (*déraison*).

43

Historical Conceptions of Madness

From Foucault's rich and unwieldy work on madness can be derived, as one of several sub-themes, the story of a gradual shift from one notion – insanity as unreason (*déraison*) – to another one, more 'civilized', more clinical and less humane – insanity as madness (*folie*).

It will be sufficient for my purpose here to treat Foucault's analysis as reflecting different images or analyses of an unvarying phenomenon – call it insanity, call it madness, as you will.[1] What is important in his account is that this condition came to be seen as sharply demarcated from the normal and sane unreasonableness of ordinary, imperfectly rational thought. Insanity was earlier regarded as a species of illogicality.

Under the influence of developments in medicine, this identification was lost. As Foucault (1961, p. 107) puts it, speaking of the experience of madness in the seventeenth century,

> Meaningless disorder as madness is, it reveals, when we examine it, only ordered classifications, rigorous mechanisms in soul and body, language articulated according to a visible logic. All that madness can say of itself, is merely reason, though it is itself the negation of reason

Between the creation of the Hôpital Général in 1657 and the liberation of the chained inmates of Bicêtre in 1794, he comments (p. xii):

> . . . something happens whose ambiguity has left historians of medicine at a loss . . . the transition from the medieval and humanist experience of madness to our own experience, which confines insanity within mental illness

The history of madness in Europe since the dark ages falls, on a superficial analysis, into two great categories. In the medieval world madness was explained religiously, as we saw. It was a form of demoniac possession and a kind of sin whose treatment, undertaken by spiritual authorities, was religious rite. With the rise of secular society a new understanding of madness emerged, developing alongside the nascent science of medicine. Rather than a moral condition, madness came to be seen as something analogous to a physical disease – an unwanted and alien visitation on a victim more pitiable than blameworthy. The history of madness, it may be said, is the history of a phenomenon understood in terms of two important models – the religious one which held sway until the end of the middle ages and the medical one which emerged and has dominated almost without challenge until the present time.

Belying this superficial duality, however, is Foucault's intricate history of insanity 'in the Age of Reason' with its analysis of the structures of madness from the medieval period to the beginning of the nineteenth century. What happened between the end of the religious understanding and the full flowering of the medical one is Foucault's concern. He charts the emergence of the medical viewpoint as it gradually crystallized out of the earlier ideas.

Foucault introduces the concept of *unreason* to characterize an image of madness which followed the religious understanding of earlier medieval or 'Gothic' thinking. It flourished briefly during the late sixteenth and early seventeenth centuries, only to be lost – or at least diluted – with the 'Classical' experience of madness in the eighteenth century. Influenced by and stimulating the 'Great Confinement', as Foucault names the secular trend towards hospitalizing and institutionalizing society's misfits which gathered pace by the middle of the seventeenth century, other images came to crowd out and eventually replace the idea of madness as a failure of reason. Inexorably, by the nineteenth century the experience of madness became entrapped in the notion of illness.

Compared with the earlier religious view of madness which prevailed for hundreds of years, or with the clinical and medical images dominating our understanding of it for the last two centuries, the image of madness as unreason gripped Western understanding only briefly. It appeared for those few years between the end of the sixteenth century and the middle of the seventeenth, then it was gone. Yet while it prevailed for so short a time, Foucault seems almost to applaud this window on madness. The voices of madness, to use his metaphor, were 'liberated' by the Renaissance and by this experience of madness as unreason, only to be silenced by the later understanding of the eighteenth century.

I too am attracted by the notion of madness as unreason, for it suggests an understanding of madness which better accords with certain beliefs we have about that condition than does either the religious or the medical conception. My interest in the history of madness, however, is entirely philosophical: I am constrained neither by the relative brevity of the structure of madness as unreason which Foucault describes nor even, indeed, by the historical accuracy of the account he offers, which has been questioned (Middelfort, 1981; Stone, 1982). While Foucault's ideas provide the initial source of the concept of unreason central to my positive thesis, my approach is entirely ahistorical and shares little with that employed in Foucault's early works to which I appeal. It is Foucault's view that the historian of ideas or 'archaeologist' alone has a role to play accounting for social phenomena like insanity: that of describing the interplay of events and ideas at some given moment in history. However, I do not share Foucault's assumptions. Our selection of an understanding of madness will be influenced by the historical context of the late twentieth century, granted. It is possible, nevertheless, to choose and justify preference for one analysis or model of madness over another, and to explore the structures of the past for hints of alternative perspectives to adopt. We need not wait passively, it seems to me, for the arrival of the archaeologists.

One further disclaimer is required. We receive, in Foucault's work, short and shadowy glimpses of the concept of madness as unreason and no sooner does it emerge in his story than it is gone, transformed by later structures. Thus what follows is no more than an interpretation of Foucault's analysis, and I must claim all the liberties of the interpreter. Not only is the thesis of less than major significance to Foucault's overall work. In addition, it is nowhere expressly formulated as a thesis in the manner in which I shall now present it, and my interpretation may not accurately reflect the role of unreason which Foucault would wish to stress.

Foucault's Unreason

Foucault makes a number of points about the image or structure of madness as unreason. First, he places it historically by reference to that emphasis on the human mind and the power of reason which gave its name to the era. The Age of Reason, during which madness was unreason, was one in which the concept of reason dominated, explained and shaped all understanding. He describes the madhouse (Foucault, 1961, p. 36), where each form of madness 'finds its proper place':

> . . . all this work of disorder, in perfect order pronounces, each in his turn, the Praise of Reason

Tamed, classified and understood, now that the trend towards confinement has instituted the madhouse, madness now

> takes part in the measures of reason and the labour of truth

It plays, Foucault continues,

> on the surface of things and in the glitter of daylight, over all the workings of appearances, over the ambiguity of reality and illusion, over all the indeterminate web ever rewoven and broken, which both unites and separates truth and appearance

Its link with dreams and illusions is at the heart of this understanding of madness, as the latter quotation suggests. The illusory, says Foucault (1961, p. 34), is itself 'the dramatic meaning of madness', and in madness

> equilibrium is established, but it masks that equilibrium beneath the cloud of illusion, beneath feigned disorder; the rigor of the architecture is concealed beneath the cunning arrangement of these disordered violences. The sudden bursts of life, the random gestures and words, the *wind of madness* that suddenly breaks lines, shatters attitudes, rumples draperies – while the strings are merely pulled tighter – this is the very type of baroque tromp-l'oeil. Madness is the great trompe-l'oeil in the tragicomic gestures of preclassical literature

Tied to this notion of madness as the other side of truth, reason and reality, Foucault seems to hint that there was, in a way, another kind of knowledge which it provided and a 'truth' in some ways more profound than that revealed by logic, the '. . . paradoxical truth of madness'. Thus he speaks of a secret delirium, underlying the chaotic and manifest delirium of madness (p. 97), a delirium which is

... in a sense, pure reason, reason delivered of all the external
tinsel of dementia ...

and the character of the Fool or Madman, he explains (p. 14),

[is no longer simply a ridiculous and familiar silhouette] ...
[he] stands center stage as the guardian of truth .... If folly
leads each man into blindness where he is lost, the madman,
on the contrary, reminds each man of his truth

Madness was a failure of reason within the person. It was 'an
intense movement in the rational unity of soul and body' and
understood within the confines of the individual. However, this
movement (p. 93)

escapes the reason of the mechanism and becomes, in its
violence, its stupors, its senseless propagations, an *irrational*
movement

Because madness was a failure of reason and something experienced by everyone, Foucault (1961) suggests, it was understood
as essentially human and explicable, rather than removed and
alien. There comes to be (p. 26)

no madness but that which is in every man, since it is man
who constitutes madness in the attachment he bears for
himself and by the illusions he entertains

One metaphor for this reduction of madness to human scale is
that of taming. The terror elicited by earlier religious conceptions
of madness as a supernatural and inhuman force is extinguished,
and madness is 'tamed' with the humanizing understanding of
madness as unreason. In the earlier period, man's dispute with
madness (p. xii)

... was a dramatic debate in which he confronted the secret
powers of the world; the experience of madness was clouded
by images of the Fall and the Will of God, of the Beast and
the Metamorphosis, and all of the marvellous secrets of
Knowledge

But with the understanding of madness as unreason, in the sixteenth and seventeenth centuries, which Foucault (1961, p. 26) describes as 'pre-classical'

> madness is not linked to the world and its subterranean forms, but rather to man, to his weaknesses, dreams, and illusions . . . [madness] no longer lies in wait for mankind at the four corners of the earth; it insinuates itself within man, or rather it is a subtle rapport that man maintains with himself

As madness was scaled down to human weakness, so – Foucault claims – it came to be identified with all human weakness. Thus came what for us today is the puzzlingly undifferentiated Renaissance concept of folly, which refers to assorted forms of error and foolishness, both those for which we naturally would hold the agent responsible and those for which we would not. Madness is folly, and human error is madness (p. 26):

> So many forms of madness abound there, and each day sees so many new ones born, that a thousand Democrituses would not suffice to mock them

Now, interestingly, the question of culpability somehow disappeared – what explained or was responsible for each folly ceased to matter, so central and familiar these conditions had become.

> A long series of 'follies', which stigmatizing vices and faults as in the past . . . no longer attribute them all to pride, to lack of charity, to neglect of Christian virtues

as they had done in the earlier period under the influence of a religious understanding of madness. Instead, they came to be attributed to (p. 13):

> a sort of great unreason *for which nothing, in fact, is exactly responsible*, but which involves everyone in a kind of secret complicity [my emphasis]

Thus, both in the preceding religious understanding of madness and in the subsequent medical understanding which prevails today, the question of the source or cause of madness was central. However, when madness was unreason it was understood more by its manifestations than by its explanation.

The very idea of unreason is difficult now for us to understand, Foucault maintains, influenced as we are by contemporary medical structures in which the force of madness lies in its being an alien, determined phenomenon – a visitation caused in the madman, reducing him to the unfreedom of the beast. Today madness is 'understood' causally. (We do not understand it. Rather, we *place* our puzzlement in an ignorance of its causal explanation.) It shows us, he says,

> nothing more than the natural constraints of a determinism, with the sequences of its causes . . .

and it frightens today because the nature of its causes renders us its victims (p. 83):

> It is a threat to modern man only with that return to the bleak world of beasts and things, to their fettered freedom

Madness is no longer understood in terms of its manifestations. The unreasonableness of the insane is now only one of several indications of their state. In the earlier structure of insanity as unreason, no deterministic explanation was invited, no unfreedom suggested; madness did not 'disclose a mechanism'. Rather, it 'revealed a liberty'. It was not a question of tending towards determinism but of 'being swallowed up by a darkness' (pp. 83–4).

Before its nature as a mechanism came to be emphasized, the unreason of madness was at its heart, serving to define and to identify it. Unreason had then, as Foucault puts it, a *nominal* value. It 'defined the locus of madness's possibility'. Only '. . . in relation to unreason, and to it alone' (p. 83) could madness be understood.

In the following chapters I shall develop and expand upon certain of these aspects of the concept of unreason which Foucault's patient 'archaeology' has revealed. Of others, I shall say no more. Because my endeavour is philosophical rather than historical, I am not obliged to respect the exact concept Foucault describes and, therefore, I shall select only certain features of that concept and graft a new notion of unreason on to them.

Of particular importance, from the point of view of the explanations which follow, will be three aspects of the earlier concept of unreason.

First, but related also to the latter point, I shall develop Foucault's notion that unreason stresses the manifestations rather than the causal explanations of madness. I shall adopt an account of madness as unreason, in which it is the unreasonable psychological functioning and not the cause or causes of that functioning which receives emphasis.

Secondly, while not equating madness with *all* human error, or 'folly' in the sixteenth-century sense, I shall stress the ordinary and familiar quality of madness which the emphasis on its manifestations as *unreasonable* brings out. I shall do this to show up a weakness of the medical model which an unreason analysis is better able to avoid: its tendency to rarefy madness and alienate its sufferers.

Thirdly, I shall return to Foucault's discussion of the central link between madness and the unreason of dreams and illusions and suggest that we should appeal to the elements shared by dreams and illusions in order to understand the kind of illogic in psychotic thought processes. I will deal with this in Chapter 6. The first two points I will take up here.

The Manifestations of Madness

My account concerns what I shall call the *manifestations* of madness, not its underlying causes. The manifestations of madness are what can be readily known of it – the psychological states and behaviour of its sufferers. Since the notion of physical disease is that of an underlying malfunction with more easily observable signs and symptoms, the manifestations of madness are what would constitute, on a disease analogy, the 'signs' and 'symptoms' of the condition.

There is a parallel here which may elucidate my stress on the manifestations of madness. Human moods, as distinct from emotions, are recognized and identified by the way in which they present themselves rather than by their causes (or, indeed, their objects). Pervasive and nebulous moods like those of sadness,

angst, and gaiety are apprehended phenomenologically in ourselves and behaviourally in others, even though their causes are
usually unknown. These, then, are phenomena which are
described in terms of what might be called their manifestations,
rather than their causes. In somewhat the same way, I wish to
restrict my discussion of the experience and nature of madness.

It follows from what I have just said that there is no incompatibility between the unreason analysis I am proposing and the
various causal explanations offered for madness in psychological,
social, genetic or biochemical terms. Unlike certain anti-psychiatry writers who propose psychological and social rather than
organic causes for insanity, I am not offering an explanation at
that level. The nature of the underlying causes of madness is not
an issue I am able – or want – to address. It is precisely my
contention in this book that these causes are irrelevant to the
important moral and philosophical dimensions of madness.

Notice, however, that the analysis offered here is not a
behaviourist one. The manifestations of madness include the
psychological states as well as the behaviour of its sufferer. An
analysis of madness in terms of its behavioural expressions would
have one severe drawback: it would not permit us to distinguish
the insane person from the impostor who merely wished to
appear insane.[2,3]

The analysis of madness offered here then is not incompatible
with the organic causal explanations usually associated with a
medical analysis. However, my proposal is that an unreason
analysis of madness must replace the medical one in moral and
legal thinking, to which the influence of the medical model has
been unjustifiably extended. In addition, my analysis may also
suggest new directions and constraints for treatment and therapy,
although the proper alleviation of the suffering madness occasions
is not an issue which I will address here.

The Ordinariness of Madness

One of Foucault's suggestions is that the adoption of a medical
model alienated the insane and rendered madness strange and
unfamiliar. This was only partly true. As the insane were 'tamed'
and lost the terror they had held for the sane, Foucault indicates,
they did become – in certain respects – less unfamiliar. Yet despite

these trends, the mad today are alienated, apart, subject to isolating social attitudes and less familiar on balance, than they were during the 'preclassical' period when insanity was unreason (*déraison*).

The criticism that medical thinking about madness has alienated its sufferers and thus perpetuated and even initiated inhumane attitudes towards them is a standard one voiced by anti-psychiatry followers. I wish to examine it here briefly, both to introduce a disclaimer about my own position and to offer a further argument in support of the unreason analysis.

One point emphasized by Foucault requires little demonstration. Madness today is a removed and puzzling phenomenon which strikes perplexity, fear, suspicion and unease in the sane. Moreover, this alienation is a social evil whose mitigation must be welcomed. The cruel and archaic attitudes of earlier times have been replaced, it is true, by a more humane sense that the mad person is not to be blamed for his or her condition, or even for the actions it occasions. Still, to suffer madness today is to suffer as much – many anti-psychiatry writers would say more – from the social and professional treatment meted out to the insane as it is to suffer from mental disorder. Social attitudes towards madness which stem from its conception as unfamiliar and removed from ordinary human experience ought to be altered.

While the medical model, through serious effort to understand madness, attempts to alleviate suffering and the lifting of moral blame is rightly represented as having enhanced the mad person's lot, it is also guilty of ignoring and obscuring the sense of madness as an unpuzzling feature of ordinary human life. Identifying and controlling the 'disease' has cast its sufferers as 'the other'. The introduction of widespread professionalism into the management of madness has increased our sense of the insane as unlike ordinary sane people whose deviations – unreasonableness, strange ideas, and excesses of feeling – we think of as like enough to our own weaknesses to be dealt with as normal human conditions. As madness became what it is today – obscure, puzzling and remote from everyday human experience – something was lost.

By introducing an unreason analysis and rejoining the links between the saner weaknesses of other people and the unreason of the insane, we might hope to recapture this sense of its ordinariness in a way that the medical model has failed to do. And reclaiming madness as a familiar human phenomenon has an importance, it must be stressed, which is more than theoretical. The proponents of the anti-psychiatry movement have recognized that the improved social and professional responses to the insane, which we would all desire, rest on this increased understanding. To see madness as more centrally connected to everyday life and experience in this way is crucial for altering social attitudes towards it.

However, social change does not require that madness and sanity be equated. Here my thesis must be sharply distinguished from an anti-psychiatry stance which bears some similarity to it. I would not suggest that sanity is itself madness – or madness sanity – or that there is no real difference between these two states. Madness is not merely in the eye of the beholder.

Rather, it is a phenomenon different and distinguishable, at least at its extremes, from sanity. The unreason of madness does share similarities with the want of reason found in sane adults, but differences still separate madness from sanity. Indeed these differences between sanity and madness are so great, I am arguing, as to serve as the basis for our moral intuition to subject the insane to radically different treatment from the sane in legal and judicial contexts.

The sane have the ability to avoid errors of judgement and action: the power to engage in the kind of scrutiny, reflection, checking against earlier experiences and against others' reactions which would allow them to do so. (This is not to say that they always do. The sane too fail to exercise this ability – sometimes they are unable to and at other times self-indulgence or self-deception interfere.) In contrast, the exculpating unreason exhibited by the insane results from an inability to avoid such errors. Due to the pervasiveness of their confusion and disorder the insane are precluded from engaging in the kind of routine reflection and checking described: their errors cannot be anticipated, isolated and prevented to the same extent as can those of a sane person.[4] The defects the insane exhibit rob them of the powers the sane enjoy, as we shall see when we examine characteristic thought processes of major mental disorders. Because it is so pervasive, their unreason is unavoidable – and, as such, exculpating.

On the one hand the adoption of the medical model has divorced madness from sanity while on the other hand anti-psychiatry seeks to equate the two. My view differs from both of these. It is that the insane are distinguishable from the sane – but in ordinary and familiar ways which we can understand. Recognition of the ordinariness of these differences should be sufficient for more humane treatment.

What must be considered now, however, is the general plausibility of treating madness as a form of irrationality or unreason, which I shall take up in Chapter 5.

This is a thesis which requires careful demonstration, despite its initial obviousness and even triviality, due to two particular trends in thinking about madness which must be handled in two further chapters. From anti-psychiatry has come the view that there is more sense in the apparent irrationality of the insane than a superficial analysis would allow. This position, associated with the writing of R. D. Laing, will be dealt with in Chapter 6. Further difficulty for the thesis comes from orthodox abnormal psychology, moreover, which has emphasized than no mere cognitive analysis captures the vagaries of madness; madness, it is claimed, is emotional and experiential as much as cognitive, so that a 'mentally sick' person may demonstrate reasoning and thought processes which are unimpaired. The weakness in this account will be discussed in Chapter 7.

Notes

1 My formulation is one which betrays the spirit of Foucault's approach, but I will not characterize the transition he documents the way Foucault himself does, as one from the occurrence of unreason to that of madness, when these are distinct phenomena. From contemporary descriptions of aberrant conditions at the time with which we are concerned, like those to be found in Weyer's writing (especially Weyer, 1563; Burton, 1621) and in the recently unearthed clinical records of Richard Napier made between 1597 and 1634 (in MacDonald, 1977), there seems evidence to suggest that in the manifestations of madness – how the mad person acted and thought – the unreason of the sixteenth and seventeenth centuries was in many important respects parallel to the madness of today. My contention that an unvarying phenomenon remained constitutes, then, an assumption – but one which is not baseless.
2 A committed behaviourist will think that in theory even the psychological states are behaviourally analysable but such a view has been disputed and need not concern us here.
3 At a practical level, of course, this is a problem for which a non-behaviourist account is equally unhelpful: we have no effective way, so far at least, to distinguish those who are shamming, whichever account is adopted. However, in theory at least, the non-behaviouristic analysis permits the distinction.
4 This is not to say that they always err any more than the sane person's ability means that he or she never does.

5
Irrationality and Unreasonableness

At the core of the unreason analysis of madness is one notion: that the manifestations of madness are characterized by an illogic and unreason related to the ordinary and familiar unreasonableness of everyday life.

This is an idea to which much superficial assent is given. It is evidenced in the easy way we substitute 'sane' for 'rational' and 'insane' for 'irrational' and in the commonplace view that sanity and madness reflect each end of a continuum and are distinguished merely by degree. However, it is a thesis, I would insist, which has been trivialized and – especially in the light of the kinds of attack to which it has been subjected in recent years – one which wants for a systematic and thoroughgoing analysis. The particular parallels which hold between everyday illogic and the thought patterns and behaviour of the insane must be explored.

Irrationality, Unreasonableness and Unreason

A want of reason is most commonly described in English as irrationality or unreasonableness, but neither of these concepts taken alone exactly conveys what we require here. Indeed, English with its two expressions seems to conceal similarities between the want of reason exhibited by sane and mad people. The breadth of Foucault's term 'unreason', which covers both the idea of irrationality and that of unreasonableness, is better suited to the concept introduced here and will be adopted in subsequent discussions.

How is the notion of unreasonableness related to that of irrationality? In general, 'unreasonableness' seems to be an ascription reserved for milder departures from reason than the term 'irrational'. The latter extends to cover extremes: the very unreasonable and perhaps even the compulsive or the totally deranged. Moreover, there are instances of irrationality where unreasonableness would not be ascribed. To give away more than one can afford is unreasonable, but to destitute oneself is not, it is irrational. Similarly, the term 'irrational' seems too strong to describe many common ways in which we show a want of reason: self-deception, impulsiveness, holding inconsistent beliefs, exhibiting weakness of will, or drawing conclusions on the basis of insufficient evidence. Only a persistent and extreme exhibition of such traits in the face of opportunity for correction deserves the title of irrationality – by which point 'unreasonable' seems hardly strong enough.

With Gallic economy, *déraison* must carry both of the notions we have been considering. In the same way I want to use the term 'unreason' to point to the less severe want of reason captured by the notion of unreasonableness as well as to the more serious failings described as irrationality. If 'unreason' is treated as equivalent to 'irrational', the severity of the deviations exhibited in madness can be acknowledged. And that severity must not be underestimated. Yet by choosing to use the notion captured in the English 'unreasonableness', it is also possible for us to emphasize and highlight the link between ordinary sane ways in which a want of reason is exhibited and their parallels in the irrational behaviour of insanity.

A second factor inviting the use of 'unreason' in preference to the more familiar terms 'irrational' and 'unreasonable' concerns a connotation shared alike by the latter two terms. 'Irrational' and 'unreasonable' – as, indeed, 'rational' and 'reasonable' – are ascribed primarily to sane adults who, it is presupposed, are *responsible* for their want of reason in a way that children and the severely deranged are not. Moreover, this feature of ascriptions of irrationality and unreasonableness to sane people carries with it a negative tone: the irrational and unreasonable are judged the worse for their weakness.

It may be argued then that these terms are not rightly, or not without confusion, used to describe the want of reason of the insane and children about which no negative judgement could be reasonably intended. And it seems appropriate to adopt the new term 'unreason' and the adjective 'unreasoning' in describing the want of reason shared by the sane, children and the insane alike.

With the aim of illuminating the shared unreason of sanity and madness, I shall first describe certain of its familiar forms in everyday life and then show their parallels in insanity. After the discussion in this chapter and the next two I shall eschew the terms 'irrational' and 'unreasonable' in favour of 'unreason'.

Definitions of Irrationality

Several distinct and important traditions have shaped our present day understanding of the notion of irrationality as that term is used in discussions of insanity. Three of these deserve particular attention.

(1) The first appeals to a notion of rationality whereby rational or reasonable acts are those based on good reasons – justified beliefs and desires which have been acquired in accord with the laws of logic and evidential reasoning. An irrational or unreasonable act then is one which was not based on good reasons. The compulsive stealing of the kleptomaniac who has no reason for what he does would be a case of irrational or unreasonable action according to this formulation; so too would action based on false beliefs maintained in the face of available countervailing evidence, as some psychotic delusions seem to be. The way a belief is formed and held, not its truth or falsity, determines its irrationality or unreasonableness with this notion. One may be unjustified in holding a true belief and unjustified in holding a false one. Moreover, the exact nature of the relationship between psychological states (of belief and desire) and action is critical: one might act irrationally or unreasonably in doing Y while holding a justified belief in X (which *would* be sufficient to rationalize taking that action), unless the action was based on, or occasioned by, the belief.

(2) The second tradition appeals to the notion of rational action as that which will maximize an agent's expected utility. Irrationality now is a relative and subjective notion and an action is irrational to the extent that it fails to satisfy the agent's subjective desires. The compulsive stealing of the kleptomaniac is also irrational according to this formulation. The action (stealing) fails to maximize the agent's strongest desire (to avoid doing so). The kleptomaniac is irrational whichever formulation is adopted and in general this will be true; those actions which maximize the agent's desires will be those based on good reasons.

(3) Finally, in reaction to limitations thought to inhere in each of these formulations there is a tradition which makes appeal to the content as well as to the mere form of the beliefs and desires marked as rational or irrational. Irrational beliefs and desires are characterized as those which are in some way – socially, morally or conceptually – unacceptable. Action based on a merely unusual belief, however well grounded, or on an unusual desire is irrational. This is a broader notion of irrationality which encompasses actions not judged irrational according to the two earlier formulations.

Discussions of irrationality and unreasonableness in this work will fall loosely into the first tradition outlined, even though it is more customary, in speaking of the irrationality associated with mental disturbance, to appeal to the third, broader kind of formulation. However, the latter is weakened because it invites the charge of arbitrariness and normativism. Granted, certain linguistic intuitions invite its adoption; but I shall show that we may account for all the kinds of irrationality in madness *important to the issue of exculpation* without appeal to it.

According to the formulation of irrationality or unreasonableness followed here, *irrational or unreasonable actions* are those not based on well-grounded psychological states of belief and desire: thus 'irrational' and 'unreasonableness' cover (1) failing to act on reasons and (2) failing to act on good reasons. Particular psychological states of belief and desire are sometimes irrational, or at least unreasonable, when they are (a) ungrounded (a hunch would be an example of such a belief; a sudden whim to act 'for no reason' or merely because one 'felt like it') and (b) not well grounded, or not based upon good reasons, beliefs and desires which comply with established rules of logic and evidence.

Irrational behaviour

Unreasonableness would hardly be attributed to behaviour alone; it seems clearly to concern the relationship between psychological states and behaviour. Although less obviously, irrationality also is rightly seen as a function of that relationship. Despite a loose and careless tendency to describe mere behaviour as irrational, irrationality is never accurately ascribed to what people do taken in isolation from their psychological states. While the behaviour of the insane, particularly, is often bizarre and seemingly irrational, we know that given some particular set of beliefs and desires any behaviour can be demonstrated to be perfectly rational. If I believe myself to be followed by an agent sufficiently dangerous, to use the simplest example, furtive and suspicious actions are appropriate and rational. If I know and suddenly remember someone to have a contagious disease, then my abrupt avoidance of their embrace makes sense.

In the early writings of R. D. Laing and his followers, much emphasis is placed on this point (Laing, 1959, 1961; Laing and Esterson, 1964). Laing's 'existential–phenomenological' analysis reveals the meaning and purpose in apparently inexplicable speech and action. His method is to postulate and ascribe to the schizophrenic a set of beliefs and desires which, if they were present, would count to 'rationalize' the behaviour exhibited rather as Freud's postulation of unconscious mental states served to rationalize the apparently irrational and meaningless behaviour of his neurotic patients. The psychological states Laing introduces are sometimes confirmed or corroborated by the patient's history or subsequent behaviour. However, like Freud he places heavy reliance on coherence of the whole achieved by this rationalization.

Laing's method can be seen in his discussion of a young patient described by the great nineteenth-century clinician, Kraepelin. On coming in, Kraepelin writes, his patient

> . . . throws off his slippers, sings a hymn loudly, and then cries twice (in English), 'My father, my real father!' . . . He does not look up even when he is spoken to, but he answers beginning in a low voice, and gradually screaming louder and louder. When asked where he is he says, 'You want to know that too? I tell you who is being measured and is measured and shall be measured. I know all that, and could tell you, but I do not want to'. When asked his name he screams, 'What is your name? What does he shut? He shuts his eyes. What does he hear? He does not understand; he understands not, How? Where? When? What does he mean?'

Disagreeing with Kraepelin, who presents the boy's behaviour and speech here as unintelligible, Laing writes that there are two ways to view it:

One may see his behaviour as 'signs' of a 'disease', or one may see his behaviour as expressive of his existence. The existential–phenomenological construction is an inference about the way the other is feeling and acting

What is the boy's experience of Kraepelin, Laing (1959, pp. 29–31) asks?

He seems to be tormented and desperate. What is he 'about' in speaking and acting in this way? He is objecting to being measured and tested. He wants to be heard

Laing's dramatic explication of madness has revealed as mistaken an ascription of irrationality on the basis of behaviour alone. (Although emphasising the 'rationality' of madness in this way, Laing's approach has served also to conceal important ways in which the insane are correctly said to be wanting in rationality, as I shall show in Chapter 6.)

Irrational and Unreasonable Persons

When persons as distinct from (their) particular actions, beliefs and desires are said to be irrational or unreasonable the terms are often used dispositionally to indicate that those persons persistently respond irrationally in at least one of the ways described (holding irrational beliefs and desires or engaging in irrational actions). In addition, there are other ways in which persons are said to be irrational: when they entertain a large number of significant beliefs and desires which are conflicting or incompatible; and when they fail to revise their beliefs and desires in the light of available evidence to the contrary and other known possibilities.

Irrationality and unreasonableness are perhaps most commonly attributable to the faulty judgement which accounts for irrationally and unreasonably held beliefs and desires as well as the resultant irrational and unreasonable action they occasion, and these will be dealt with in Chapter 6. However, before turning to these forms of irrationality and unreasonableness, I wish to consider other ways in which persons and their actions may be irrational and unreasonable.

Impulsiveness, *Akrasia* and Unconsciously Motivated Behaviour

Three familiar forms of unreasonableness found in otherwise sane people are described here; each one, it will be shown, bears similarities to forms of unreason found in insanity.

In impulsiveness an action of some consequence is taken in the absence of a reason or known reason for it, or a reason sufficiently substantial and considered for the occasion is acted upon. Buying an expensive luxury on the spur of the moment might, for a poor person, count as such an impulsive action. If not judged irrational, having such a sudden whim at least would be judged unreasonable.

The action must be one of some consequence: impulsive action insignificant in its consequences is likely to be dismissed as neither reasonable nor unreasonable. Tossing a stone in a pond, or choosing a drink – these actions are often impulsive but are not naturally classified as to their want of reason because they are unimportant. (Another exception of this kind is non-empirical beliefs. Those, it will be shown in Chapter 6, are similarly exempt from judgements as to their rationality or lack thereof.)

In *akrasia*, or weakness of will, inclination conflicts with obligation so that, while the agent believes he or she has better reasons for doing X than Y and is not physically or psychologically prevented from doing X or forced to do Y, he or she deliberately does Y. I promise myself that I will put down the novel at the end of the chapter in order to attend an important meeting, and I fail to do so. Given my obligation to attend the meeting, my inclination to continue reading seems insufficient reason to miss it: thus I follow my inclination against my better judgement.

In impulsiveness and akrasia there is a logical disparity between psychological state(s) and behaviour. The psychological state (the absence of any adequate reasons for acting in the case of impulsiveness and the presence of an overriding obligation not acted upon in that of *akrasia*) is insufficient to illuminate the action undertaken. This lack of logical fit must be distinguished from the explanatory disparity suggested by the theory of unconscious motivation. According to that theory, a person may act on a motive not consciously entertained, producing instead a 'rationalization' which he or she believes (falsely) to explain what he or she was doing. A generous gesture is made, for example, out of nothing more than an unconscious wish for attention.

The disparity here is not logical. Its logical fit with the behaviour it is falsely believed to have occasioned is precisely its *raison d'être:* only because the action was consistent with a motive of generosity could that particular rationalization have persuaded its author. The reason offered, or rationalization, is sufficient to make sense of the behaviour but not the reason for its having occurred, and thus is insufficient for its complete explanation.

An explanatory disparity such as this between psychological states and behaviour would sometimes be described as unreasonable, or even – depending on its severity – as irrational, just as would the logical disparity in impulsiveness and *akrasia.*

Compulsive behaviour, for example, where a person's beliefs and desires all support one course of action and yet that person persistently does another, is analogous to *akrasia.* The notion of compulsion is a complex one and will receive further analysis in Chapter 9. It is sufficient here to recognize that the tendency towards compulsive behaviour defines one common kind of mental disturbance (Compulsive Personality Disorder) and is a central characteristic in those others classified as disorders of impulse control such as kleptomania.

An example of compulsive behaviour is that of the hand-washer described in the following case (Cameron, 1963, p. 392), who must continue the practice even while acknowledging her hands to be perfectly clean and her skin painfully damaged by her rigour.

> Sally returned home . . . with a fully developed handwashing compulsion which did not go away. She soon had an ugly, painful dermatitis . . . ugly and painful or not, the hands and forearms had to be scrubbed every time Sally went to the toilet and every time she had a 'sensual sensation' or thought about contamination

This is behaviour which would naturally be described as irrational rather than as unreasonable on account of its severity. Yet it seems apparent that it is related to the unreasonable *akrasia* described earlier, where I could not resist reading even though to do so was to miss a meeting I wished to attend. Like the sane person succumbing to weakness of will, the compulsive hand-washer has no reason – or not a sufficient one – to act as he or she does.

In a similar way, ordinary impulsiveness is related to the more extreme 'impulsiveness' suggested by some accounts of schizophrenia. Despite the emphasis placed on the rationality of much apparently bizarre action, Laing, for example, describes cases where behaviour in no way connects with thought. We are close here to the picture of the raging lunatic, or to use Laing's own metaphor, of the divided self: a whole without a central intentional core to perform the integrating task which alone could yield logically related thought and action. In his famous analysis of the case of a schizophrenic girl, Julie, Laing (1959, p. 195) writes of a stage in her disintegration when, in being with her,

> One had for long periods that uncanny praecox feeling, described by the German clinicians, i.e. of being in the presence of another human being and yet feeling that there was no one there

The praecox feeling, he remarks, should be the audience's response to Ophelia:

> Clinically she is latterly undoubtedly a schizophrenic. In her madness, there is no one there. She is not a person. There is no integral selfhood expressed through her actions and utterances. Incomprehensible statements are said by nothing. She has already died. There is now only a vacuum where there was once a person

In ordinary impulsiveness, we saw, action fails to reflect thought. Parallel – although vastly more extreme – is the failure of Ophelia's action and words to express the intentional psychological core which Laing calls 'integral selfhood'.

Finally, the relatively insignificant and isolated instances of unconscious motivation thought to mark the sane and even the mildly neurotic person are matched in the severely disturbed – according to psychological theories derived from psychoanalytical thinking – by behaviour which is extensively understood in terms of the person's unconscious psychological states. The following account (Crowcroft, 1967, pp. 118–19) of psychosis reveals the way unconscious processes are introduced to explain such conditions as schizophrenia.

> The schizophrenic disassociates part of his ego from himself. This is an unconscious process, however, and he does not realise that the voices he hears originate within himself. Much that is unconscious in us becomes conscious in him. Yet he does not recognise himself and his own past experiences in his present hallucinations, even though the voices often seem to come from his own head . . . . He fails to realise that his altered sensations are a result of 'hallucinatory wish-fulfilment'; and that his strange sexual excitements, and the altered smells, tastes and feelings in his body all originate from aspects of himself which have become alienated from each other

The irrationalities of the sane attributable to the effect of their unconscious life seem in many respects the same as those of the insane although they differ in their significance and frequency.[1]

What emerges from this look at some disparities between psychological states and behaviour is that, while the more severe of them and those we would perhaps more naturally describe as irrational are associated with mental disturbance, they are related to and may be regarded as extensions of patterns which are found in sane people acting unreasonably.

Each of these cases of irrationality and unreasonableness might be analysed as particular actions taken without, or with insufficient, reasons. There are also ascriptions of irrationality and unreasonableness to persons as distinct from their particular actions: entertaining inconsistent beliefs and clinging to beliefs in the face of countervailing evidence.

Entertaining Inconsistent Beliefs

The tendency to entertain *inconsistent* beliefs and desires invites ascriptions of irrationality, as was noted earlier, when these states are significant ones and there are a number of them; lesser failings of this kind, moreover, would probably be said to be unreasonable; and such inconsistency is a feature both of the sane and of the insane person. It is illustrated vividly, for example, in the self-deception of everyday life. Here, one belief is held simultaneously with another conflicting one where there seems to be recognition of their incompatibility. An example might be that of a person's believing a desired outcome would occur even while knowing of evidence proving such an eventuality impossible: she believes her daughter will get well while knowing the affliction from which she suffers to be an incurable one.

Less puzzling inconsistencies also, when they persist, are judged irrational or unreasonable. There are, for example, those due to a failure to recognize the incompatibility between several beliefs and desires held simultaneously. I might believe that every creature has a right to life and form the desire for a pair of leather gloves, as long-lasting and warm, failing to realize that the manufacture of leather gloves – requiring as it does the violation of that right in some animals – conflicts with the belief that every creature has a right to life. This may be sheer oversight, not self-deception – although if it is prolonged, such 'oversight' becomes suspect as a case of self-deception.

Paralleling common self-deception, some forms of madness may themselves be understood as extremes of self-deceit. This comparison becomes more obvious, perhaps, if the Freudian notion of repression is substituted for that of self-deception – which it seems in important respects to resemble. At least in dynamic psychology repression is used to explain extreme cases of derangement – dissociative states, for example, like those of psychogenic amnesia or multiple personality – as well as the less severe sort of case described above where a mother deceives herself over her daughter's condition. Consider the following account (Sarason and Sarason, 1980, p. 152) of psychogenic amnesia.

A young man dressed in work clothes came to the emergency room of a hospital in the city in which he lived with the complaint that he did not know who he was. He seemed dazed, was not intoxicated, and carried no identification. After being kept in the hospital for a few days, he woke up one morning in great distress, demanding to know why he was being kept in the hospital and announcing that he had to leave immediately to attend to urgent business.

With recovery of his memory, the facts related to his amnesia emerged. The day his amnesia began, he had been the driver in an automobile accident that resulted in the death of a pedestrian. Police officers on the scene were convinced that the driver had not been in the wrong: the accident had been the pedestrian's fault. The police told the driver to fill out a routine form and to plan on appearing at the coroner's inquest. The man filled out the form at the home of a friend, accidentally left his wallet at his friend's home, and mailed the form. After mailing the form he became dazed and amnesic. He was led to a hospital by a stranger. The amnesia was probably related to the stress of the fatal accident, fear of the inquest, and worry that he might actually have been responsible for the accident

The parallel between this massive amnesia and more isolated forms of forgetting is obvious. Self-deception or repression, whichever terminology is favoured, it seems appropriate to describe a person suffering from these extreme conditions as entertaining inconsistent beliefs and desires and to speak of this man, in particular, as both knowing and not knowing his own identity. At a less dramatic level, such inconsistencies are noted in conditions like depression where, quite typically, the depressed person believes both that he or she is worthless and insignificant and that he or she is fated for special attention and treatment, perhaps by God. This appears to be the same kind of inconsistency as is exhibited, to a lesser extent, in a sane person's deceiving herself over the fatal nature of her daughter's disease.

Clinging to Beliefs

A second way in which persons as distinct from their particular actions, beliefs and desires may be irrational or unreasonable, it was seen, involves a failure to revise beliefs and desires in the light of evidence. We are familiar, in everyday life, with the tendency to maintain or adopt beliefs and desires on the basis of insufficient support: to cling to some ideas, failing to revise them despite available – even obvious – evidence, or holding them without adequate grounds when some would be required. We have no hesitation in judging a person who does so with some persistence as less than rational or reasonable. This is a common trait, seemingly stemming as much from inertia as from positive reasons to 'favour' the beliefs or desires in question – the same reasons inviting the self-deception described earlier.

With the particular weaknesses described here we enter the realm of *faulty judgement*, for a person who is irrational or unreasonable in this way exhibits a weakness of reasoning. However, this trait requires separate attention from the other forms of faulty judgement to be explored in Chapter 6, on account of its close resemblance to manifestations of derangement about which certain misconceptions must be averted.

In madness, the equivalent of this everyday weakness is delusional thinking. Delusions are defined, in psychiatric symptomatology, as false beliefs persistently held in the face of inadequate evidence or evidence supporting a contrary conclusion, and they are portrayed as features common to all severe mental disturbances. Indeed, on first appearances it would seem that the tendency towards delusory thinking must be one of the most salient ways in which the mad person exhibits irrationality.

This supposition, however, is somewhat misleading. The 'delusions' of the mentally disturbed are not as reliable an indicator of a want of reason in this sense as their technical definition suggests; in fact, it is often doubtful whether, according to that definition, what the insane person suffers are rightly described as delusions at all. For with the curious exception of pure paranoia, to be dealt with in Chapter 7, delusional thinking is accompanied by a failure to 'test reality' – to distinguish hallucinated from verdical experience. And if a person suffers from an apparently delusional belief and maintains it despite reassurances to the contrary, it may be that doing so is based upon idiosyncratic but countervailing 'evidence' provided by hallucinations. Consider the following passage (Sechehaye, 1951, p. 170) from the autobiography of a schizophrenic girl plagued by imperious demands from 'The System', an inner voice urging self-destructive action upon her.

> I had, too, the conviction that my behaviour was deceitful. In reality, it wasn't anything of the kind. I was deeply sincere. But if I disobeyed the System to maintain the integrity of my

personality, I was deceitful since I acted as though I had no consideration for the order. If I obeyed it, I was equally deceitful, since I did not agree to burn myself. I suffered horribly from the orders and from the feeling of treachery so contrary to my character

Despite her therapist's persuasion this patient maintained a belief in her own deceitfulness. What counts, here, as evidence of the girl's sincerity? If we consider only the objective or public evidence – the reassurances of her therapist that she has done no wrong – then indeed it would be true to see the girl's belief in her deceitfulness as irrational and delusory. But what of the idiosyncratic 'evidence' concerning the System? Because her refusal to obey the demands of the System provided, for her, *grounds* to maintain the belief – grounds, moreover, which in their force and insistence over-rode the objective evidence to the contrary – we cannot simply judge hers as a case of refusing to alter a belief in the light of countervailing evidence.

Nor is this an isolated case – although for further instances of this problem of classification we must turn not to psychiatric case studies but to haunting autobiographical accounts of madness like the one quoted, where a private hallucinated world is revealed.

To summarize: if delusions are merely taken to be false beliefs, delusional thought is not irrational as such – for it may be false but well-grounded. If by delusions we mean the stronger notion of holding beliefs without respect for evidence, then it is not so clear that delusion is widespread among those suffering psychotic states. The insane may be somewhat more vulnerable to true delusion than are the sane, but the presence of delusional thinking cannot be appealed to *in any general way* to demonstrate this kind of irrationality in insanity. The widespread ascription of delusion to the insane does not immediately establish their want of reason, and we must explore further for that evidence.

The irrationality and unreasonableness which is found in the sane and the insane alike may be summed up as comprising two elements: holding and acting upon insufficient reasons (which includes clinging to unwarranted beliefs and desires in the face of countervailing evidence) and entertaining inconsistent beliefs and desires.

To capture the further notion of *exculpating unreason* by which unreason counts as an excuse, two additional features must be added. These tendencies are more pervasive and widespread in the thought and action of the insane and of children, and consequently the insane and children are less capable of avoiding them than are ordinary sane people who exhibit the same or similar tendencies. These features of exculpating unreason will be established in Chapters 6 and 7.

Note

1 They also differ in other respects, of course, at least in Freud's formulation of the distinction.

6

Hallucination and Thought Disorder

In this chapter schizophrenia and psychotic thinking will be explored in the light of two aspects of everyday life: faulty judgement and the experience of dreams and illusions. Unlike the kinds of everyday unreason described previously, dreams and illusions are not instances of irrationality and unreasonableness as such, of course. But they are a kind of non-rational, erroneous experience with important and useful reflections in the experience of psychosis. By showing parallels between these two everyday experiences and those of the schizophrenic, I shall hope to reveal and emphasise the commonality between sanity and madness and to provide a view of madness less puzzling than the usual one conveyed by a medical model.

Two claims for the supposed rationality of madness will also be addressed here: that of Laing and certain empirical investigations on the logic of schizophrenic thought which might be taken to invite a similar conclusion to Laing's. In each case, I shall insist, misapprehension rests on a failure to appreciate the breadth and diversity of unreason.

Faulty Judgement

Sometimes beliefs are loosely described as unreasonable or ir-rational solely on the basis of their content, i.e. what are the beliefs about? Strictly speaking, however, not the content of a belief but the manner in which it was formed or is held should determine an assessment of its rationality or reasonableness. If it is a well-grounded belief, then it will be rational or reasonably held; if not, then it is wanting in one of these ways. Just as any behaviour can be rationalized given a certain set of beliefs and desires, so the content of almost any belief can be rationalized given a certain account of its acquisition or maintenance. Even the most unlikely beliefs *may* be reasonably held – as, indeed, may beliefs which are erroneous. If the road sign is altered, and those I ask along the way lie about my direction, then I have reason to believe – and reasonably believe falsely – that I am reaching my destination when I am not. Given an extensive enough network of deception practised against me I could have reason to believe all sorts of falsity.

So a well grounded belief is not to be treated as equivalent to a true one – although it is generally assumed that by conforming to the laws of logic and of evidential reasoning, i.e. by being possessed of well-grounded beliefs, we put ourselves in the best position to hold a maximum of beliefs which are true.

Another connected qualification must be made here. Ascriptions of reasonableness, unreasonableness, rationality and irrationality in sane people are largely restricted to those beliefs for which standards of correct reasoning procedure are available. We enjoy more latitude with regard to the way we hold and come by metaphysical and religious beliefs, for example, than we do empirical ones because there are not agreed upon evidential rules for assessing the reasonableness and establishing the likely truth of such nonempirical claims. When they are entertained by otherwise sane people, such nonempirical beliefs are generally held exempt from ascriptions of unreasonableness and irrationality. The widespread belief in an after-life, for example, would be judged unreasonable only by the most stringent adherent to naturalism.

This exception seems to indicate that the unusual religious and metaphysical beliefs characterizing psychotic states of mind cannot rightly be treated as the source of an ascription of irrationality to them. The orthodox belief in human immortality differs from the schizophrenic's messianic belief that she has been chosen by God for some special task only in respect of its widespread acceptance. If the one is not to be judged as irrational, due to the absence of agreed upon evidential rules guiding the acquisition and holding of such beliefs, then neither – it would seem – should the other. There are important differences between the thinking of the deranged person and the sane one, which do warrant the ascription of a greater degree of unreason in the former. However, these differences cannot be found in the content of nonempirical beliefs held by the deranged – even though the bizarre, unusual and all-absorbing quality of these metaphysical and religious beliefs often constitute the most immediately apparent feature of their madness. The differences on the basis of which the ascription of unreason is rightly made to the insane, as we shall see, concern a want of reason in the way beliefs are formed and held.

The illogicalities and unreasonableness of everyday sane thinking are legion and familiar. By these standards we are not, as humans, very rational creatures at all. One small part of our everyday want of reason shows itself in invalid reasoning, where the rules of deductive logic are transgressed but in addition the fallacies of less formal logic are regularly committed – for example, those of ambiguity where, in the Fallacy of Equivocation, we confuse the different statements a given sentence may be used to make and form a fallacious argument by equivocating upon them. Finally, our inductive or evidential reasoning is subject to error in countless ways: we jump to conclusions, we over-generalize in ways which are unwarranted, we fail to connect and draw conclusions which are indicated, and we persist in holding beliefs without sufficient evidence, in the way discussed in the previous chapter.

Such faulty judgement is found alike in practical and in non-practical reasoning. It is when action or behaviour reflects unsound practical reasoning that ascriptions of irrationality or unreasonableness are perhaps most common. Much reasoning is practical; it is directed towards action. Thus rationality is sometimes formulated as acting so as to maximize an agent's expected utility and this designates a species of practical reasoning whose conclusion is,

X will maximize my expected utility so I should do X

This formulation expresses a common theoretical interpretation of the notions of rationality and irrationality outlined in Chapter 5.

Not all reasoning, however, is practical, and the acquisition of a person's beliefs and desires is judged independently of their role in practical reasoning. This point may be illustrated by what is presented (Maher, 1966, p. 88) as a typical schizophrenic thought pattern, where it is reasoned,

. . . General Eisenhower is a veteran. My therapist is a veteran. Therefore my therapist is General Eisenhower

The patient to whom this sequence is attributed then addressed his therapist as 'General', saluted him when they met and stood at attention in his office. The patient's behaviour – taken alone – seems bizarre, but the fault does not lie in his practical reasoning. Given his belief that the therapist was Eisenhower, his actions were not inappropriate. Errors of judgement may occur, then, both in practical and in nonpractical reasoning.

Dreams and Illusions

Let us consider the second kind of everyday experience with parallels to madness: dreams and illusions. Dreams and illusions are experiences where, to use Descartes's phrase, our senses deceive us. We are led into error and false judgement because we have them. And these commonplace occurrences reveal a kind of experience which is akin, in certain ways, to that of the psychotic.

The content of dreams has long been acknowledged to reflect a want of reason. Freud, for instance, quotes Cicero: 'There are no dreams that are *absolutely* reasonable and that do not contain *some* incoherence, anachronism or absurdity' (Freud, 1900, p. 88).[1] There may be meaning in the illogic of dreams, as Freud has argued, but as they present themselves they are deeply nonrational. Moreover, Foucault's intriguing epigram whereby the illusory is the 'dramatic meaning of madness' (Foucault, 1961, p. 34) invites, I suggest, that we also regard our everyday experience of illusion – being tricked by the mirage, seeing the straight stick in water as bent, hearing the distant sound as loud in humid weather – as akin to the unreason of madness.

Psychotic Language and Thought

Some of the apparent illogicality of psychotic thought emerges in the following quotation (Cameron, 1963, p. 566) from a woman at the height of a manic episode.

You go and stand pat, pat, you hear? Who was Pat? What does he wear when he's in Ireland? . . . See this (raised pillow behind her head)? Now is it even or odd? Even or odd, by God? By God we live; by God we die. And that's all my allegiance to these United States. See my little eagle (bed sheet wrapped around her feet and stretched taut)? These are my wings. No, I have wings of a girl . . .

It is evident also in the following passage (Maher, 1966, p. 426) written by a man diagnosed as schizophrenic,

If things turn by rotation of agriculture or levels in regards and 'timed' to everything; I am re-fering to a previous document when I made some remarks that were facts also tested and there is another that concerns my daughter she has a *lobed* bottom right ear, her name being Mary Lou . . . Much of abstraction has been left unsaid and undone in this product mild syrup, and others, due to economics, differentials, subsidies, bankruptcy, tools, buildings, bonds, national stocks, foundation craps, weather, trades, government in levels of breakages and fuses in electronics too all formerly 'stated' not necessarily *factuated*

(Neologisms, or newly coined, idiosyncratic words and phrases are here emphasized.)

However, difficulties confront us in using writing and speech to establish the illogic of insanity. First, at its most deranged the mind resorts in its expression to 'word salad', neologisms and incoherent babble – or there is silence. Yet in illustrating deranged thought, speech with at least minimum coherence and intelligibility must be used. One risk here is that the resultant picture of insanity will be distorted by exclusive reliance on atypical cases – those where some coherence and language is preserved.

More serious is the problem of whether words like these actually express the thoughts they appear to. Clinical experience has been understood to confirm that they do (Brown, 1973). However, we know from the speech disorders of those suffering certain kinds of known brain dysfunction that speech is not always a reliable indicator of thought. Those who have limited lesions in the left hemisphere from a stroke, for example, will continue to perform well on the nonverbal portion of an intelligence test, suggesting the absence of any cognitive impairment to match their verbal and linguistic difficulties (Gardner, 1974).

Moreover, there is a sceptical hypothesis which has at times been asserted concerning psychotic speech in particular. Laing (1959) has suggested that schizophrenics are especially motivated to conceal their thoughts. Thus, if he were right, we should have more than the usual doubts as to whether schizophrenics mean what they say. This hypothesis will be considered in more detail presently, but it will be shown to be unproven, even unprovable. And until some firmer evidence of a parallel between schizophrenia and the organically produced aphasia described earlier can be discovered, we may reasonably proceed despite these potential impediments. Recognizing that it is an assumption, and acknowledging that limitation, I shall assume that schizophrenics' 'thoughts' find expression in their words in the way that their words would seem to indicate.

The Schizophrenias

The central place which the schizophrenias must take in any discussion of madness derives from their status as psychotic disorders. In psychiatric nosology, the more general category of psychosis is standardly distinguished from neurotic disorders and personality disorders by its severity and by the distinctively psychotic failure of 'reality testing'. There are other border-line conditions whose classification as neurotic or psychotic is disputed (paranoia, for example), just as there are those whose classification as insanity is in doubt (like addiction). However, the schizophrenias count as central cases both of psychosis and of madness.

Moreover, most of what is important to us in schizophrenic thought holds true also for other psychotic states, such as manic and depressive reactions. The thought disorder and failure of reality testing characterizing the schizophrenias are attributes shared among the psychoses. Since it will be these with which we are primarily concerned – rather than, for instance, the characteristic content of the schizophrenic's beliefs – an analysis of the schizophrenias will also serve to illuminate other psychotic states.

The schizophrenias are defined in the following way by the American Psychiatric Association (1980, pp. 120–1) in the Glossary from the *Diagnostic and Statistical Manual* (DSM III) which represents the standard medical psychiatric orthodoxy:

a large group of disorders, usually of *psychotic* proportion, manifested by characteristic disturbances of language and communication, thought, perception, affect and behaviour which last longer than six months. Thought disturbances are marked by alterations of concept formation that may lead to misinterpretation of reality, misperceptions, and sometimes to delusions and hallucinations. Mood changes include ambivalence, blunting, inappropriateness, and loss of empathy with others. Behaviour may be withdrawn, regressive, and bizarre

Of the five areas of disturbance listed here (language, communication, thought, perception and affect), I shall concentrate on two: thought and perception. Some of my rationale in doing so is based on the assumption that words reflect thoughts. Disturbances of language and communication count as secondary effects of the more fundamental cognitive disturbances. Perceptual disturbances are also central since they affect the acquisition of the set of beliefs most subject to evaluations of rationality and reasonableness: empirical claims.

The schizophrenic hallucinates; also he or she is described as suffering disturbances of thought, or what is sometimes referred to as 'thought disorder'. One is a disturbance affecting perception while the other is a cognitive failing. Yet the two are not as unrelated as at first appears and as clinical descriptions (including the one just quoted) usually imply. We will look at each in turn.

Many attempts have been made to describe and isolate the characteristic processes involved in the thought disorder marking these conditions (see Pavey, 1968; Seeman, 1970; Mayer, 1972). The predominant approach in studies during the last 80 years has centred on the schizophrenic's associative capacity *vis-à-vis* particular concepts and words, and involves attempts to prove that 'schizophrenics are confused about the meanings of words' as one study puts it (Schwartz, 1978, p. 239).

One widely used descriptive category in these studies is that of *over-inclusion*, a term introduced to describe the failure to isolate the intended or appropriate associations of a concept or idea from its unintended or inappropriate ones. This involves both a failure to sift out the appropriate one from a word's several 'public' uses, or what might be called its intersubjective content, but also a failure to distinguish the personal and subjective connotations of concepts and ideas from their public or intersubjective ones.

Although they have mostly suffered from methodological weaknesses[2] studies conducted since the beginning of this century, and particularly during the last 30 years have seemed to indicate the presence of a significantly greater degree of over-inclusion in the thinking and speech of schizophrenics than in normal control groups (Schwartz, 1978). Among other things, schizophrenics are less likely to separate out the arbitrary, personal cluster of associations which come to mind along with the general meaning or meanings of a concept – i.e. that part of its meaning which is shared among other language users.

Other studies have described and attempted to account for thought disorder in other ways (Schwartz, 1978) but I shall concentrate on this tendency towards over-inclusion. Not only has it received a great deal of attention experimentally but, more importantly, it may be understood as related to a general tendency towards confusing fantasy and reality, which also explains the perceptual disorders known as hallucination, and thus links the two broad features of perceptual and thought disorder. This link is suggested in the following passage from a psychiatric text (Maher, 1966, p. 412)

> In language and thought, the schizophrenic is not able to keep his responses to the external world separate from the fantasy processes that are going on at the same time. His behaviour, especially his language, thus presents a picture of frequent interruptions. As these interruptions are also in the form of words, the total effect is of long sequences of disorganized and bizarre communication, some elements of which are responses to his environment and some of which are determined by fantasy

The first sentence of this quotation expresses a standard way in which psychotic states are distinguished from the less severe neurotic ones. Due to a tendency towards hallucination, psychotic states are said to be marked by a failure of *reality testing*, which is usually understood as an inability to distinguish false from veridical perceptual experiences and beliefs.

What is hallucinated is not merely what is false, however, as the quotation indicates, but also what is fantasied. The schizophrenic's beliefs and ideas are unrealistic not only in being false – which they undeniably are – but in being subjective, rather than public or intersubjective. When this is emphasized the separation of defects of perception (hallucination), from defects of thought and reasoning (over-inclusion), seems an artificial one. We can recognize that it is as much the reality of intersubjective meanings as of sensory items which the schizophrenic fails to 'test'. It is not reality in the sense of some objective standard of truth which fails to be acknowledged; it is rather reality in the sense of the features which are shared between other thinkers and perceivers – the aspects on the basis of which there is public agreement in judgement.

The schizophrenic's failure to test reality reflects an important difference from the way in which sane people hold beliefs and register experiences. In sane thinkers idiosyncratic connotations are distinguished from intersubjective ones; an idea's subjective associations are effortlessly separated from its public *meaning*. Moreover, the sane person's perceptual experiences are, in general, shared, thus perceptual beliefs correspond. This is an aspect of ordinary experience and thought so obvious as to go un-noticed and unremarked. Yet it is one, I would argue, whose insignificance belies its importance for our status as reasonable creatures.

This idea may be illustrated if we compare the schizophrenic's disorder with dreams and other common illusions. When as sane and wakeful people we fall prey to perceptual illusions we too, like the hallucinator, sometimes fail to distinguish what seems to be from what is. The stick seems bent in water; it is not. However, here the illusion is not, in general, idiosyncratic: any naive perceiver placed in the right position would draw the same erroneous conclusion. There is – or is the possibility of – agreement in judgement over how the bent stick seems, albeit that how it seems is not how it is. Illusions, unlike dreams to which we shall turn next, are usually shared or sharable false images. This I take to be part of what we intend by the term 'illusion': when the sane – from tiredness, stress, or drugs – experience false images which are unsharable in the way described, they too hallucinate. Were they to do so with the regularity of the schizophrenic and without any recognition of the particular conditions producing and cir-cumscribing their aberration, they too would have lost their ability to test reality.

Similarly, there are people whose specialized knowledge permits them to have experiences which we do not have, as has been remarked (Coulter, 1973). The trained observer can see Sirius in the night sky while most people cannot, for example. These experiences are merely unshared, however, not unsharable. I too could see Sirius by studying astronomy, i.e. by studying procedures which are known and understood. Intersubjective agreement, as I am using the expression, implies the presence of a sharable, though perhaps not shared, experience.

The false images of madness, in contrast to true illusions, are doubly erroneous: they are untrue and, more importantly, they have not the validity of intersubjective agreement.

Foucault (1961, p. 104) seems to imply the latter distinction when he speaks of the madman's mind as being

> . . . on the one hand . . . led on by the oneiric arbitrariness of images, on the other, and at the same time (imprisoned in) the circle of an erroneous consciousness

The difference between the common experience of illusion and a psychotic failure to test reality then is fundamental. The illusion of the sane person invites a false judgement. However, psychotics are more than imprisoned in erroneous consciousness, as Foucault puts it: they are also alone in their error, solipsistically alienated from the world of intersubjective meanings by the 'oneiric arbitrariness' of their experience.

We will now examine dreams. Illusions, we have seen, are false but not idiosyncratic or 'arbitrary' (Foucault): the error is shared or sharable. On the other hand, it may be said that dreams are both erroneous and unshared in the moment we experience them. With dreams, however, we know on waking the twofold nature of our error. I dream of a house which is not there. On waking I relinquish both my false belief in its existence and the strange concentrated meanings with which, through the processes Freud (1900) describes as condensation and displacement, I have embued it. The hallucinator, in contrast, recognises no such reliable return to a common reality, unless of course the 'symptoms' subside spontaneously or from chemical intervention. (However, in the latter case the person is no longer insane. Only a medical understanding of madness obliges us to see the temporarily sane person as a schizophrenic in remission.)

Yet despite the differences between schizophrenic experience and the common experience of dreams and illusions, the similarities can also inform us. Because we – the sane – know illusion, we understand hallucination even if we have not experienced it in one of the particular conditions described above (tiredness, stress, or drugs). The experience of dreams remembered is of images false and idiosyncratic – only recognizably so. Every sane person is acquainted in retrospect with this twofold experience of psychosis. The experiences differ in critical respects but there are undeniable parallels between them.

The ordinariness and familiarity of madness to which I have been pointing is implied, I think, in Foucault's assertion that madness *is* illusion. The illusory, he declares, is itself 'the dramatic meaning' of madness (Foucault, 1961, p. 34). At least, it seems true that the schizophrenic's oneiric images and subjective meanings have clear reflections in the experience of the sane person.

A failure to test reality by not distinguishing subjective from intersubjective experience and meanings, moreover, must be seen itself as a very fundamental want of reason – one so fundamental that its absence is presupposed in the laws of logic and evidence. It is more than a mere failure to reason well in some particular respect: it is that without which reasoning could not occur. Language based upon intersubjectively shared meanings constitutes the building blocks of discourse and communication, for which in turn are required agreements in judgement, in Wittgenstein's phrase (Wittgenstein, 1953).

The schizophrenic's thought indeed bears close similarities to what Wittgenstein describes as a private language. Wittgenstein raises the impossibility of a private language to demonstrate the absurdity of a misleading picture of our knowledge of sensations: the view, in particular, that because sensations are not publicly observable they are named by something like private ostensive definition. He invites us to imagine such a naming process and then argues that whatever 'names' resulted would fail to be part of any real language.

Wittgenstein has been read to offer several different objections to the idea of a private language, each of which may be usefully related to thought derived from the idiosyncratic meanings and experiences of the schizophrenic. One rests on the impossibility of verifying the consistency of a sensation 'language' such as that described: there could not be a private language, he seems to suggest, because there could be no way of finding out whether a term was being used (by the same person) on several occasions to refer to the same sensation. It is the hidden nature of sensations, in particular, upon which this argument rests (Wittgenstein, 1953, sect. 243–81).

Another objection asserts that having a language is a form of following a rule. Following or failing to follow a rule involves consistency with, or divergence from, what a number of people do. Thus there could not be a language for one person only, whether it was a language of sensations or of anything else. Moreover, what it is to act in accordance with a rule cannot be determined by the arbitrary stipulation of rules, even by a group. Rather, it presupposes agreements in judgement between people, so that the standard of correctness rests, finally, upon what people do naturally: their shared responses. Without these shared responses and shared 'forms of life', there would be no language (Wittgenstein, 1953, sect. 138–242).

When the schizophrenic hallucinates and does not distinguish public from private meanings, his or her 'language' (or better, speech since he or she has no language or thought), is private in both the ways implied in these arguments. The objects of his or her 'thought' have the privacy of sensations because they are not connected in any apparent and predictable way with public, external events or stimuli and because he or she does not share with others the responses, the forms of life, which are required for a shared language.

A 'private language' like the schizophrenic's speech is hardly a language, and certainly 'thought' undertaken in it could not rightly be described as rational or reasonable. The minimum requirement of having reason – without which we can reason neither well nor ill, neither logically nor illogically – would seem to be communicable thought. Communicable thought, which presupposes the ability to test reality, is the basis upon which the application of logic proceeds. Thus a shared intersubjective language is a presupposition of logic and reason.

The unreason in madness lies in the privacy of its 'language'. And this conclusion helps to illuminate Foucault's remark that language is the first and last structure of madness (Foucault, 1961, p. 100). It is the idiosyncrasy, the oneiric quality, the privacy of the 'language' of the psychotic which is at the heart of insanity:

If the determinism of passion is transcended and released in
the hallucination of the image, if the image, in return, has
swept away the whole world of beliefs and desires, it is
because the delirious language was already present [my
emphasis] – a discourse which liberated passion from all its
limits and adhered with all the constraining weight of its
affirmation to the image which was liberating itself. . . . It is
in this delirium, which is of both body and soul, of *both
language and image*, of both grammar and physiology that
all the cycles of madness conclude and begin

I have been considering the schizophrenic's tendency towards
over-inclusion from the broadest possible perspective. The more
narrow hypothesis that schizophrenics break the laws of formal
logic to a notable degree is one which has received attention in
experimental psychology. In a famous study by Von Domarus
(1944, p. 111), schizophrenic mental activity was defined in terms
of the presence of certain kinds of logical error, and described as
'paralogical' and 'pre-logical'. Thus:

> Whereas the logician accepts only the Modes of Barbara or
> one of its modifications, as a basis for valid conclusions, the
> [schizophrenic] paralogician concludes identity from the
> similar nature of adjectives . . . and accepts identity based
> upon identical predicates

Even 'logicians' are guilty of some illogicality of this kind, of
course – a point obscured here – so it is a difference of degree
which is hypothesized. However, subsequent testing failed to
confirm even the supposition that such illogicality is relatively
more common in the paralogician. When schizophrenics were
matched with a normal control group on tasks involving syllogistic reasoning, they failed to reveal a significant difference
between the normal tendency to reason illogically and the
schizophrenic's habits (Williams, 1964).

With that, Von Domarus's hypothesis was summarily dismissed, and the supposition adopted that the schizophrenic is as
logical as are sane adults. Yet experimental findings have
repeatedly confirmed the presence of over-inclusion in schizophrenic thinking. In both verbal and nonverbal test tasks,

schizophrenics have been shown to fail to sort and distinguish classes and concepts as well as a normal control group because of a seeming failure to apprehend and distinguish intersubjective meanings and experiences from private ones (Maher, 1966).

The tension between these two findings invites a re-evaluation of empirical psychology's understanding of the notion of illogicality. It is the narrowness of that understanding which accounts for the disparity, I suggest. Nonrationality shows itself in more than the ability to discern formal invalidity in syllogistic reasoning. The categories of fallacious reasoning established by logic fail to capture over-inclusion because it is more, and more deeply, nonlogical than the laws of logic – established on the vast 'logic' of sane thought – were formulated to address. Without some distortion, I think it impossible to show over-inclusion as fallacious reasoning. It can be argued, for example, that the over-inclusive thinking of schizophrenia is itself an extreme instance of certain kinds of informal fallacy of ambiguity and relevance. But this very approach seems misdirected in failing to acknowledge the breadth of illogic in over-inclusion. It is the very presuppositions of logic and rational discourse – more than any particular logical rules – which are violated by the schizophrenic's 'private language'.

There seems to be evidence to confirm that the thought processes of the insane are less influenced by logic and reason than are those of a sane adult. However, this conclusion must now be set against Laing's stress on the rationality of madness.

Laing's Rational Schizophrenics

The kinds of unreason explored in this chapter have to be emphasized because of the influence of certain tenets of anti-psychiatry. Laing was concerned to 'rationalize' seemingly unintelligible behaviour, as was shown in Chapter 5, and the effect of his emphasis is not to be denigrated. In addition, he has suggested other analyses by which the schizophrenic might be seen as rational – in initially choosing madness over sanity, for example – although some of these claims have recently been questioned (Brown, 1976). I do not wish to challenge all the ways in which madness may reflect reason, however, but rather to correct a legacy from thinkers like Laing: the widespread false impression that overall, and in the most significant sense of that term, the mad person is as rational as anyone.

Part of my disagreement with Laing's views rests simply on his neglect of other obvious senses in which the insane are more irrational than are sane people. However, one of the ways in which he attributes reason to the schizophrenic offers a more direct challenge to the claim of errors of judgement I have been emphasizing: the supposed rationality of speech understood as expressive action. As a means of *expressing* inner states, it is suggested, the apparently incoherent speech of the schizophrenic is appropriate and reasonable. In discussing the patient described earlier, whom Kraepelin interviewed, Laing (1959, p. 30) remarks:

> [he] is carrying on a dialogue between his own parodied version of Kraepelin, and his own defiant rebelling self. . . . Presumably he deeply resents this form of interrogation which is being carried out before a lecture room of students

The man's action is characterized here as a purposeful one whose goal is the expression of his resentment over the way he is being treated and, were the account accurate, it would rightly be said to have some minimal rationality. However, there is a difficulty with Laing's interpretation. The man's strange speech *may* serve to express his inner states, it is true, but this claim must be distinguished from the one that it does so *in order* to express them. Beliefs and feelings are sometimes expressed unwittingly, when they are, however, their expression is neither rational nor irrational. The difficulty here is that neither Laing's discussion nor the description provided by Kraepelin makes it clear whether the expressive act is of this unwitting kind or is a purposeful one. [This point has been made by Brown (1976) in his comprehensive critique of Laing's various assertions on the rationality of schizophrenics.]

Moreover, even if we concede that practical reasoning has taken place so that the speech is minimally rational in being undertaken purposefully, for a fuller rationality it must be shown why more conventional means would not better express the inner feelings. The man could say 'I deeply resent this form of interrogation', for example, and this would seem both a more direct and a more forceful means of expression.

Elsewhere, Laing describes the responses made to his psychiatrist by another schizophrenic patient who afterwards recounted the interview to him, and here he does succeed in providing reason for the patient's indirection:

He thought the psychiatrist more and more a fool. The psychiatrist asked him if he heard a voice. The patient thought what a stupid question this was since he heard the psychiatrist's voice. He therefore answered that he did, and to subsequent questioning, that the voice was male. The next question was, 'What does the voice say to you?' To which he answered, 'You are a fool'

By playing at being mad in this way, Laing concludes, the patient had contrived to 'say what he thought of the psychiatrist with impunity' (Laing, 1959, p. 164). The patient can show his disgust with the psychiatrist without insulting or annoying him. Thus, were the patient's expression of his feelings the only purpose of his speech, it might be possible in this case to concede, with Laing, that it counted as rational in some fairly strong way.

However, we use speech purposefully to bring about other ends than self expression: most commonly we use it to communicate. If such were the purpose of the speech in this case, its rationality again comes into doubt. Laing omits to say whether his patient understood the end to which the psychiatrist's clumsy questions were directed. Let us assume, as he seems to imply, that the patient was aware of the psychiatrist's wish to discover whether auditory hallucinations were experienced. If so, then it would seem that acknowledging the intent behind the question and answering it directly and straightforwardly would have been a more rational way of achieving the goal of communication.

Moreover, there is an additional problem for Laing's hypothesis. His insistence that the schizophrenic has the added motive of concealment carries the ring of the *post hoc ergo propter hoc*. If the schizophrenic is motivated to conceal his thoughts – including, presumably, his motives – then his or her statements about them would be unreliable – leaving us without a means of direct confirmation for the accuracy of his or her claims.

In summary, Laing's hypothesis concerning the rationality of schizophrenic speech presents difficulties at several levels. It may be questioned whether these statements are purposive at all and thus can be judged as rational or irrational. Then we must question whether, if they are, they are not considerably less rational than available, alternative courses, both in bringing about (1) the simple goal of self-expression, and (2) more sophisticated goals such as those related to communication. Finally, if we accept the Laingian view that schizophrenics are motivated to conceal their inner states, reliable claims by them as to the rationality of their actions would seem not only unproven but unprovable.

Insanity then, contains unreason: it involves ways of thinking and perceiving – and, as I shall show in Chapter 7, of feeling – likely to result in faulty judgements and in reasoning contrary to the presuppositions and laws of logic.

Notes

1 Nihil tam praepostere, tam incondite, tam monstruose cogitari potest, quod non possimus somniare.
2 Possible unchecked variables in most of these studies, as is shown by Schwartz (1978), include associative distraction, ignorance of the meanings of words, the rate of guess-work and the effects of psychotropic medication and hospitalization (since most of the schizophrenics studied came from hospital populations).

7
Paranoid Delusion and Affective Disorder

The delusions of paranoia and the so-called affective disorders of depression, mania and manic–depressive cycles require special attention. This is because they are central rather than border-line cases of derangement (the affective disorders reach psychotic severity and, while the status of pure paranoia as psychosis has been disputed, it was traditionally so classified), and because they may occur ostensibly in the absence of any cognitive disturbances. Affective disorders, as their title suggests, involve as their most notable feature alterations of mood and feeling rather than disturbances of a cognitive kind while pure paranoia, as we shall see, is standardly characterized by the absence of dementia (that is, defects of reasoning) and of hallucination.

The above generalizations immediately require some qualification, however. Affective disturbances occur on a scale of severity spanning from mildly neurotic to floridly psychotic. They may thus be accompanied by the thought disorder and hallucination of other psychotic reactions. So not all cases of affective disorder need concern us; some are too mild to count as serious derangement, and others too severe to present a problem of the kind described, where there appears to be affective disturbance without cognitive impairment. In what follows I shall discuss only those cases of affective disorder which are severe and yet not severe enough to exhibit the failure of reality testing characteristic of psychoses.

Similarly, what has been said about paranoia must be qualified. One type of schizophrenia is described as paranoid on the basis of the persecutory, jealous or grandiose content of the delusory beliefs maintained by its sufferers. Since in this case the typical defects of reason characterizing psychotic states will be present, it is not paranoid schizophrenia, however, about which I shall be

88

concerned. Rather, my attention will be directed towards what is sometimes called pure or classical paranoia: the condition characterized only by systematic delusions of a persecutory, grandiose or jealous nature.

On the face of things – to return to my thesis – these two kinds of condition contradict the assertion that in all severe psychiatric conditions we find particular defects of reason which could warrant our treating the insane as manifesting an exculpating want of reason. However, I shall argue that a careful look at the characteristic features of these states reveals something more. The most salient of the features distinguishing pure paranoia and affective disorders may not be a cognitive failing. Still we can see that those features would be accompanied by some defect of reasoning. Let us begin with the puzzling condition known as pure paranoia.

Paranoia

In psychiatric literature the paranoid, far from being irrational, is unfailingly portrayed as a philosopher's madman – eminently reasonable. Look first at Kraepelin's classic definition (1904, p. 145):

> . . . the insidious development of a permanent, unshakeable delusional system from inner causes in which clarity and order of thinking, willing and action are completely preserved

and commentary:

> In this disease . . . there occurs regularly a mental working up of the delusion to form a delusionary view of the world – in fact a 'system.' The disease leads to a 'derangement' of the standpoint which the patient takes up towards the events of life. . . . First, suspicions begin to appear which gradually become certainties and steadfast convictions. The delusions become connected with real perceptions and occurrences which are construed only in morbid and prejudiced ways; hallucinations never come under observations or only quite occasionally. . . . The paranoid patients are generally in a

condition without gross disturbances and still able to engage in some profitable business.

Among contemporary sources, there is the current American Psychiatric Association's definition (1980, p. 100):

> *Paranoia* A rare condition characterized by the gradual development of an intricate, complex, and elaborate system of thinking based on (and often proceeding logically from) misinterpretation of an actual event. A person with paranoia often considers himself endowed with unique and superior ability. Despite its chronic course, this condition does not seem to interfere with thinking and personality

Because of the absence of apparent cognitive disturbance, there is disagreement among those classifying paranoia as to whether it should find its place among the more severe, less reality-based psychoses, or with the milder neuroses.

The category of paranoia is quietly omitted from some psychiatric texts, moreover, and the term 'paranoid' enters as an adjective only, to describe the content of a belief or set of beliefs – as it does in the category of paranoid schizophrenia – suggesting that the very classification of pure paranoia may be a bogus one, to eventually meet the fate of other declassified conditions like that one most recently struck from the official nosology of the American Psychiatric Association – the 'sexual dysfunction' of homosexuality. However, paranoia is a condition still regularly referred to and, because of the importance of its use, I shall proceed as if it were – as the passages quoted suggest – a legitimate, if peculiar, psychiatric category.

When his or her reasoning is characterized as more rational than the sane person's, how can it be maintained that the paranoid exhibits defects of reason?

It is true that the paranoid's beliefs are described as *delusions*, i.e. as both false and maintained in the face of grounds or evidence casting doubt upon them. However, we saw in Chapter 5 that this technical concept of delusion is problematic in its psychiatric application and cannot be appealed to in any straightforward way to confirm the presence of unreason in madness. Either many so-called delusions based on the evidence provided by hallucination are not strictly delusions – the beliefs may be false but they are not ungrounded – or in psychiatric contexts the term must be taken to refer merely to the holding of beliefs which are false, regardless of their epistemological status. Construed in the latter way, however, delusion is compatible with reason; merely holding false beliefs is not as such an indication of a want of reason. Though I want to show that there is a want of reason in paranoid thinking, it is not due to entertaining delusions in this narrow sense.

Since the paranoid does not hallucinate, it is not possible to challenge the description of delusory thinking by insisting that his or her false beliefs are based on evidence from that source. However, there are analogous difficulties with attributing 'delusions' to paranoid persons, as we shall now see.

The paranoid does not hallucinate, but still there remains the suggestion in Kraepelin's commentary, quoted earlier, that however impeccable may be his or her subsequent logic, the paranoid's defect of reasoning lies in judgements made on the basis of his or her experiences. Paranoids may be supposed to reason faultily in drawing unjustified conclusions from what they accurately perceive; it may be a question of failing to weigh the evidence properly. They construe real perceptions and occurrences 'morbidly and prejudicially', as Kraepelin puts it.

Indeed, this inability to weight the evidence as most people would, seems to be an important feature of paranoid thought. A tendency to distort and exaggerate emerges from psychiatric case studies as a salient aspect of paranoid reasoning and as the basis of its description as 'pseudo logic'. This is acknowledged in the following account of paranoia from a standard text (Cameron, 1963, pp. 477–8). (The author is speaking particularly of the most common kind of paranoid delusions which are persecutory in content.) Similar claims, however, are made about other kinds of paranoia where erotic, jealous or grandiose delusions predominate.[1]

> The paranoid person is equipped with a chronic expectation that others will treat him badly or deceive him, and with a readiness to react aggressively whenever he feels badly treated or deceived . . . [he is] exquisitely sensitive to the smallest traces of hostility, contempt, criticism or accusation in the attitudes of other people. The trouble with this hypersensitivity is that it always finds something on which to

feed. All of us harbour minute traces of hostility even in some of our most favourable attitudes towards others. . . . These traces are usually unconscious and the periods of indifference unimportant. Sometimes they are momentarily conscious – a passing resentment towards a good friend, a temporary annoyance with someone we love, an occasional feeling of aloofness that we may not always recognise. . . . [The paranoid] detects our contradictory traces clearly and consciously, even when we are totally unaware of them ourselves.

Because of his selective sensitivity to slight, resentment or rejection, he greatly magnifies what he perceives. He may make a molehill of momentary dislike into a mountain of eternal hatred. He takes it immediately for granted that the traces of hostility or indifference which he detects are clear, dominant and conscious in the thought and feelings of others

So the paranoid with delusions of persecution may be described as exhibiting defective mental functioning or pseudo-logic in holding unreasonable or unwarranted beliefs and suspicions about others' attitudes towards him or her.

These distorted judgements form the basis of the paranoid's elaborately developed system. Starting from the falsity of these initial beliefs and, with ingenuity derived from their often-remarked superior integrative capacity, people who are paranoid develop the warped, systematized explanations of the world for which they are known. (Much is made in the clinical literature of the ingenuity with which beliefs and experiences are integrated into the delusory system: it is stressed as an essential aspect of paranoid reasoning. But since it is not as such a defect of the paranoid's thought processes – only a difference – we cannot appeal to this aspect of the condition to show the unreason of paranoid thought.)

While seeming to provide us with an account of the specific defect characterizing paranoia, however, the passage quoted raises further problems. Paranoids are pictured as grounding their distorted beliefs in *some* evidence. This suggests that while at least some of their beliefs may be false, they – like the false beliefs of the person subject to hallucinations – can hardly be described as delusions in the fullest sense. There may be grounds, idiosyncratic but legitimate, for maintaining these false beliefs, and these grounds may outweigh the evidence for relinquishing them. Thus, if the clinical description quoted earlier is accurate, paranoia still raises difficulties for our attempt to show the condition as one exhibiting unreason. Before examining these, let us look more closely at the kind of presuppositions entailed in that description.

This analysis of paranoid sensitivity embodies a number of the tenets of dynamic psychology, each of whose validity may be questioned. The most obvious of these presumes that there are unconscious feelings, and that these feelings are manifested in our behaviour in ways that we, and most other people, are unaware of. Only· by presupposing these can the author reason that paranoid persons are able to isolate and 'home in' on precisely those unconsciously displayed attitudes which go unobserved by most of us because they lie beneath the threshold of normal sensitivity.

While these claims are standardly accepted by dynamic psychologists, they each need a complete empirical validation, and are certainly open to doubt. However, if we suppose their correctness and accept, with the author, that the paranoid has an unusual sensitivity to negative attitudes of others, then there remain problems for the way in which the paranoid's 'pseudo-logic' is usually described. Most notably, we seem forced to question the authority of those who judge the paranoid's beliefs as unrealistic and exaggerated. This is a serious difficulty for the account of paranoia being proposed, although I shall show that it is one which is eventually surmountable. Let us examine it more closely.

The first part of the difficulty is this: from the same discussion in which the paranoid's failure to restrict himself or herself to well-grounded beliefs is described, the conclusion may be drawn that some paranoid beliefs might be said to be better grounded, in one way, than those of the sane person. Paranoids have available to them evidence from which the normal observer's relative insensitivity precludes them. The author emphasises the irrationality involved in exaggerating and magnifying what is perceived, but he admits that the paranoids' hypersensitivity to others' attitudes allow them access to existing phenomena. Though unperceived by sane people, the traces of hostility, contempt and criticism to which they are described as responding are not mere figments of the paranoids' imagination.

When we speak of a belief as well grounded or reasonable, we imply that it is based on all the available evidence and not merely that it is a sound assessment of some of the evidence. It seems that the paranoids' sensitivity permit them to have all the available evidence about others' attitudes towards themselves – although, as the passage quoted emphasizes, they then invalidate their judgements based on this evidence by distorting their conclusions so that the sane person, despite his or her relatively inadequate perceptual capacities, always reaches a more accurate assessment of others' attitudes than does the paranoid.

Yet in one way the more 'accurate' judgements made on the basis of less evidence have no more claim to being well grounded and reasonable than have the exaggerated judgements of the paranoid. Consider the following case:

The Case of Christopher's Feelings

Despite usually feeling warmly towards P & N, Christopher has occasional, short lived twinges of hostility towards both of them – twinges of which he is himself unaware. P, who is paranoid, detects these feelings, perceives and disregards the signs that Christopher feels warmly towards him, and judges his attitude to be one of dislike. N, on the contrary, fails to detect the signs of Christopher's unconscious dislike and, on the basis of the positive attitude towards him which he does notice, basks in what he imagines to be Christopher's wholehearted approval

Overall, N's judgement about Christopher's feelings towards him may be more accurate than that of P. If it is true that Christopher's attitudes towards both are mostly positive, then N's belief that Christopher feels warmly towards him is nearer to the truth than P's belief that Christopher dislikes him. But a match for P's error in disregarding the evidence of Christopher's positive feelings for him, and concentrating on the negative components in his attitude, is present in the grounds from which N draws his relatively accurate conclusion. These grounds comprise at least one false belief: the belief, based on his inaccurate perception, that Christopher feels nothing but fondness for him.

Now the second, entirely sceptical aspect of the problem emerges. Evaluations of the paranoid's judgement as exaggerated and distorted are made by psychiatric clinicians – experts of a sort in this area, although their expertise is not due to superior perceptual abilities so much as to theoretical knowledge. The psychiatrist's claim is that while the paranoids' perception is accurate, their reasoning on the basis of what they perceive is muddled – but why need that be so? It seems possible that paranoids are not guilty of exaggeration, that both their reasoning and their perception are accurate, and that the unconscious negative feelings which they detect in others are of such magnitude as to render insignificant any positive feelings towards them. Paranoids are charged with making mountains out of real molehills, but might it not be that their molehills are really mountains?

How does the perceptually insensitive psychiatrist judge between the last two hypotheses? A psychiatrist's evidence for the presence of unconscious attitudes which the paranoid perceptually discerns is, for the most part, highly conjectural, based on an interweaving of theoretical claims and his or her knowledge of the patient's consciously experienced emotions and beliefs. In the context of this discussion, however, it can be seen that these theoretical claims also must be treated as suspect, since they are inextricably bound up with the observations of perceptually insensitive observers.

Their perceptual 'insensitivity' seems to preclude the sane from the privileged position of detached arbiter as to what are realistic claims here. Their supposed epistemological advantage has been exposed and we are left with a radical scepticism. We seem forced to admit that there is no way to assess the paranoid's beliefs as rational or not.

Must we then reject the suggestion that irrationally held beliefs can be isolated in the mind of the paranoid? Must we concede that while a difference in functioning can be demonstrated a defect of the kind which could count towards regarding paranoia as an irrational condition, cannot? I shall now insist that we need not do so. It is a difference in functioning, yet it is a defect as well.

Light can be thrown on this problem by considering other peculiarities of perception analogous to the paranoid's hypersensitivity to negative feelings. A gift (although, as we shall see, defect might better describe it), in a small number of the population, is especially acute hearing. This allows the hyperacute hearer to discern sounds lost to normal perceivers; however, as an apparently contingent corollary, it affords hyperacute hearers the dubious benefit of hearing all sounds more loudly than normal perceivers do and, thus, of hearing many ordinary sounds as uncomfortably loud.

Is the hyperacute hearer placed in a position to more accurately assess real sounds? In one respect, surely we must suppose so: he or she hears sounds which are present though indiscernible to normal hearers. We should – and would – defer to his or her superior knowledge of those sounds. This corresponds to the paranoid discerning actual, though perhaps unconscious, traces of hostility. Likewise, if the feelings are there, we must defer to the paranoid's more complete account.

However, this analogy is not complete. There are several other kinds of judgement which the paranoid and the hyperacute hearer might make, and it is in looking at these that a disanalogy between the two can be demonstrated – and the unreason of paranoia revealed.

Some claims that the paranoid makes will be justified, we saw. Particular perceptual judgements, like 'Christopher now feels dislike for me' expressed by P who is paranoid, correspond to the particular perceptual claim of the hyperacute hearer – 'A sound of drum beats is coming from the direction of the Medina'.

However, the paranoid also regularly makes another kind of perceptual judgement, of a more general kind – perceptual claims about the feelings of others, summing up overall emotional attitudes: both 'Christopher's overall present feeling for me is great dislike' and 'Christopher dislikes me' intended disposition-ally. Hyperacute hearers make no judgement equivalent to these general perceptual claims. They simply hear all sounds as louder; they have no analogy to the paranoids' experience of apprehend-ing and weighing both negative and positive feelings to yield their final judgement that the negative ones surpass the positive in predominance and/or intensity. The hyperacute hearer has no direct evidence of soft sounds to correspond to the direct evidence of positive feelings which the paranoid fails to acknowledge.

In addition to these general perceptual claims made by the paranoid there are judgements which, while not themselves per-ceptual, are drawn from perceptual judgements: predictions, for example, about how others will act and intentions. 'Christopher means to kill me, so I should buy a gun to protect myself!' It is with this kind of judgement that paranoid reasoning reveals itself as irrational. Instead of accurately weighing negative against positive feelings, the paranoid ignores the latter – thus committing a standard error of theory formation whereby only some evidence is acknowledged and the rest disregarded.

With this last kind of judgement there is again some analogy with the judgement of the hyperacute hearer, who may conclude 'Don't go in there, the sound will deafen you'. If this admonition is addressed to a normal hearer it will be misleading, and may also reflect a defect of reason of a kind similar to that exposed above. True, there is no direct evidence by which hyperacute hearers can be expected to avoid the conclusion that what is painfully loud for them will also be so for normal hearers, but there might be indirect evidence: their knowledge of past instances when their perception was found at odds with others, for example, or the apparent comfort with which others were tolerating the noise. The judgement would be irrational if they failed to take into account these indirect ways of disconfirming the basic judgement that the sound is uncomfortably loud.

Moreover, a failure to acknowledge and give appropriate weight to *indirect* evidence may account for the paranoid's unreason in the conclusion 'Christopher is going to kill me': Christopher's words, behaviour and past attitude seem to be disregarded – along with the directly countervailing evidence provided by the experience of the positive feelings themselves – in the formation of the judgement.

In conclusion, it seems possible to answer the sceptical objection raised to the proposal that a specific defect – forming distorted judgements due to an oversensitivity to negative attitudes – enables us to describe the paranoid as not merely deviant in his or her beliefs but as hindered by faulty reasoning.

Like other conditions, such as depression and anxiety, paranoia seems to be found in a limited respect in sane people. Moreover, in a more general form, the kind of unreason isolated here – a tendency to distort and exaggerate claims based on perceptual experience – is one encountered in the illogicalities of everyday life.

Affective Disorders

It is the serious but nonpsychotic affective disorders known as neurotic depression and hypomania, and not the more severe psychotic reactions of depression and mania, which are central here and I shall argue that these conditions contain features likely to lead to defects of reason.

This discussion is invited by a particular problem, it will be remembered. It is not at first obvious how a cognitive analysis of madness as unreason such as that I am defending can accommodate those kinds of derangement which centrally involve noncognitive states of feeling.

Now the presence of the extreme forms of affective disorders of mania and depression which reach psychotic proportions, serves substantially to counter the problem at the outset, as was pointed out earlier. The presence of psychotic thinking exhibited by the more severe episodes of both mania and depression show the same cognitive defects which were seen in Chapter 6 as characteristic of all psychotic states. Moreover, as I shall now show, serious but somewhat milder disorders of hypomania and neurotic depression also – although less obviously – may be seen to reveal unreason.

Some of the manifestations of so-called affective disorders are recognizable as extreme forms of familiar states and dispositions (despair, sadness, hopelessness and gaiety, elation and euphoria, for instance) which we ascribe to sane people. Thus the *major affective disorders* are defined (American Psychiatric Association, 1980, p. 87) as:

> a group of disorders in which there is a prominent and persistent disturbance of mood (depression or mania) and a full syndrome of associated symptoms

where *depression* involves (p. 28):

> a mood of *sadness, despair and discouragement* (together with slowed thinking, decreased purposeful physical activity, guilt and hopelessness, and disorder of eating and sleeping

and *mania* indicates (p. 87):

> *a mood disorder characterised by excessive elation* (hyperactivity, agitation and accelerated thinking and speaking)

Cyclical conditions where mania gives way to or is followed after varying lapses of time by depression, or the reverse, differ only in aspects unrelated to our discussion (these are the so-called Bipolar and Cyclothymic disorders). Their manifestations, at any given time, resemble those of mania or depression, so I shall not treat them separately here. Nor shall I discuss the widely accepted theory which identifies manic and depressive reactions as part of the same condition. I am concerned merely with their manifestations in the sense of that term developed in Chapter 4 and my sole justification for treating the two contrasting sets of manifestations together reflects their both being affective states.

It appears to be primarily a matter of degree – both of intensity and duration – which marks off normal and familiar states and dispositions from the milder disorders of effect, described as neurotic depression and hypomania, in which we are interested here. Neurotic depression, for instance, has been described as differing from ordinary moods of sadness and discouragement in the following way (Cameron, 1963, p. 413):

> Gloomy self-deprecation becomes a *neurotic depressive reaction* when a person grows chronically preoccupied with complaints of unworthiness, failure or hopelessness, when he remains dejected in spite of everything, loses initiative and interest, and lapses into repetitive expressions of futility which his actual situation, objectively considered, does not justify. . . . The mood is not merely one of apprehension but of despair

The parallel case of hypomania, moreover, is distinguished along similar lines (American Psychiatric Association, 1980, p. 49):

> *hypomania:* def. A psychopathologic state and abnormality of mood falling somewhere between normal euphoria and mania. It is characterized by optimism, pressure of speech and activity, and a decreased need for sleep. Some people show increased creativity during hypomanic states, while others show poor judgment, irritability and irascibility

and again (Cameron, 1963, p. 560):

The grandiose delusions of mania . . . are often little more
than mere exaggerations of ordinary self-assertive pride,
boastfulness, optimism and self-aggrandizement. . . .

It is not clear that we would always want to excuse the sufferer
from non-psychotic affective disorders such as have been
described here. We are close, in such cases, to the difficult
border-lines where moral intuitions to excuse weaken and fail us.
Somewhere between the mild euphoria and the feelings of despair
and discouragement which we recognize as normal responses on
the one hand and the heights of elation and depths of misery
marking states of derangement on the other, our intuitions as to
the blamelessness conveyed by the conditions falter. Normal
moods of discouragement and euphoria do not constitute excuses
for action undertaken, and extreme and abnormal ones do, but it
would be hard to say exactly where the line is drawn.

Rather than attempting to establish that because of defects of
reason in these cases there are grounds for excuse, I shall merely
seek to show in this chapter that if there were an intuition to
excuse in cases of affective disorder then defects of reason and
reasoning could be pointed to in grounding that intuition.

Cognitive and Affective States

An analysis in terms of irrationality such as I am offering would
be classified by some as a 'cognitivist' or 'intellectualistic' one;
and it has been claimed (most recently by Culver and Gert, 1982)
that such a cognitivist analysis fails to accommodate affective
states and mental disorders based upon affective disorders. For
this reason, as I stated earlier, like paranoia the severe 'affective
disorders' – when unaccompanied by psychosis – require a special
discussion in the context of the thesis that madness is unreason.

There is a misleading presumption underlying such a claim,
however, and indeed underlying the whole system of classification by which 'cognitive' and 'affective' states and disorders are
contrasted: that affective states contain no cognitive element.

It is a misleading oversimplification to suppose that we do not
believe and think as part of feeling. It is misleading because from
the mistaken assumption that feelings do not contain or entail
thoughts derives the mistaken notion that the only aberrations or

defects in affective states are those not susceptible to a cognitivist analysis, and this is wrong.

Exploring the matter further, we shall see that much of what is affective, or to do with feeling, is also cognitive. Emotions, attitudes and desires, for example, not only contain thought but are susceptible to error in just the same way as are purely cognitive states.

It is because these states have a cognitive element that they can be (and are) assessed as rational or irrational. I shall trace the cognitive element in emotions and show how it determines our tendency to describe some emotions as irrational or inappropriate in two quite distinct ways. Then I shall show that moods such as mania and depression also contain a cognitive element which, less directly, can be pointed to in order to explain the sense in which an excessive mood of despair or elation may be said to be defective or a disorder.

We will look first at the affective conditions known as emotions and attitudes. These differ in important ways from each other but they are linked in being alike said to be intentional conditions (Williams, 1959; Pears, 1962; Kenny, 1963; Thalberg, 1964) – by which is meant at least that they contain beliefs and they are about or over something known to the person affected by them. If I am angry I know to whom or what my feeling is directed (I know the feeling's *object*, technically speaking) and I hold certain beliefs about it. Clearly, there is a major cognitive component in emotions and attitudes.

Moods, however, are less clearly cognitive. They are standardly distinguished from intentional states like emotions, precisely by reference to their failure to be directed towards a single, identifiable object. They are 'objectless' according to some theorists (Kenny, 1963; Solomon, 1977); at least their objects are not, or need not be, known to the person affected by them. Thus they contain something closer to what might be thought of as pure feeling unmixed with thought.

Many fleeting moods may indeed be entirely noncognitive. However, I shall argue that having states of despair and elation with the intensity and/or prolonged nature and pervasive quality by which the moods of neurotic depression and hypomania are marked off from normal moods of elation and despair, does involve holding certain very general beliefs. So there is a cognitive element in the moods of mania and depression, at least, if not in all moods; and that cognitive element can be appealed to in explaining the way in which these conditions are 'defective', just as the cognitive element in emotions and attitudes can explain the way that they may be irrational.

Let us look first at defects of emotion and attitude. If I am angry with X because (I believe) he did p, then the rationality or appropriateness of my anger is dependent upon the epistemological status of my belief that X did p. If that belief is well grounded then my anger is rational, or rationally justified; if not, then it is not.

This is perhaps the most obvious way in which emotions can be assessed as to rationality, but it is not the only one. Also, the kind of situation warranting emotional response of a certain kind may be characterized; for such a characterization we would appeal to that emotion's definition. Regret is standardly defined as being felt over past events. Confronted with an emotional response indicating 'regret' in the absence of the object of regret's being a past event, we would most naturally choose to withdraw the title of regret.

An alternative, with some less exactly defined emotions, might be to argue that the response was irrational. Thus the *inappropriateness* of some emotional reactions seems irrational. We do not say that the woman who titters at the sight of suffering is not amused, but rather that her amusement is irrational. This second way in which emotions may be said to be irrational is of particular importance here because it corresponds to a standard psychiatric condition – not one which is technically described as an affective disorder although, in more general terms, that is precisely what it is: the schizophrenic suffers the irrational emotional reactions so described, technically distinguished as 'inappropriate affect' and 'mood incongruence'.[2]

To understand the kind of failure exhibited by those suffering what are technically called affective disorders, we must introduce a third way in which emotions and affective states seem to be judged as defective. The manic or depressed person's response is wanting because he or she experiences a disproportionate degree of it. There is excessive elation or despair relative to the situation. The response may be well grounded and broadly appropriate to the setting in each of the two ways described above, but it is wanting in its proportion.

To see the force and significance of this judgement, we must look more closely at the kinds of condition being dealt with here. Let us begin with the clinical descriptions offered earlier. The feelings of inferiority, guilt, unworthiness and hopelessness of the person experiencing a depressive reaction, are not defective in quite the same way as those radical kinds of inappropriateness of affect found in schizophrenia and noted earlier. The text quoted indicates that there is a lack of objective support for these states, but the matter is often not so clear cut. To feel guilty, hopeless and worthless, or elated and self confident, can sometimes be warranted by the way the world is. No person is perfect in every way, for example – nor yet imperfect; no view, objectively speaking, is absolutely gloomy – or enchanted. There is often some evidence then to support different frames of mind on this particular continuum, from the blackest despair to pure joy. Freud (1917, p. 156), speaking of the beliefs of sufferers from clinical depression or melancholia makes the point well. Some of the sufferer's statements, 'we are at once obliged to confirm without reservation',

. . . in certain . . . self-accusations [the melancholic] seems to us justified, only that he has a keener eye for the truth than others who are not melancholic. When in his exacerbation of self-criticism he describes himself as petty, egoistic, dishonest, lacking in independence, one whose sole aim has been to hide the weaknesses of his own nature, for all we know it may be that he has come very near to self-knowledge; we only wonder why a man must become ill before he can discover truth of this kind

It is on a scale of intensity that the manic and depressive affective states are wanting. However, what the reasonable quantity of guilt is for a misdemeanour – perceived or real – or the right degree of exhilaration over an advantage is often difficult to say; and the rules by which the appropriate degrees of effect are laid down seem sometimes to reflect nothing more than statistical norms: what is a suitable degree of these reactions is what most people experience. Moreover, the norms themselves are highly culture specific, as has frequently been observed (Carstairs, 1959): excessive gloom in one cultural context is regarded as an even keel in another.

Thus, rather than attempting to discover a defect of some kind in the affective responses themselves which mark these conditions, I suggest instead, that these responses are likely to lead to defects of reasoning.

Unreason in Hypomania and Neurotic Depression

I will now examine more closely the cognitive element in the moods of mania and depression. The states of elation and despair, respectively, characteristic of these two conditions are distinguished from ordinary familiar states of elation and despair by their intensity and duration, as we saw earlier. The feelings last longer and are experienced more intensely in these conditions. They must then be more pervasive than ordinary moods, affecting a person's entire point of view and more completely and thoroughly colouring his or her experience than do ordinary elation and despair.

This pervasive nature of depression and mania is nicely expressed in a passage by John Custance, whose personal account of a manic–depressive condition will be explored in more depth presently. Here he describes his 'hypomania' (Custance, 1952, p. 30):

> . . . the general sense of well being, the pleasurable and sometimes ecstatic feeling tone, remains as a sort of permanent background of all experience during the manic phase

A pervasive mood of elation like that described, or one of despair, must be expected to affect action. I may experience a private afternoon of despair or joy and give not a sign, but pervasive despair and elation could be expected to show themselves in action *because they must entail beliefs.*

A disposition towards despair and a gloomy point of view, even at a normal level, involves some general beliefs which could be expected to affect reasoning – a pessimistic belief that all things being equal something will go wrong (things will turn out badly, for example) – just as a normally optimistic disposition entails believing, rosily, that they will turn out well. These beliefs do affect judgement and action. Were we confronted with persistent protestations of pessimism, misery and despair from people whose evidential reasoning and action remained unaffected by their putative affective state, we should come to doubt their sincerity (or, perhaps, their self-knowledge).

Thus even ordinary despair and elation involve, I would insist, certain very general beliefs likely to enter into reasoning. In the pervasive moods of mania and depression, these beliefs could only be more pronounced and more marked in their effects. With the distortion of persistent pessimistic or optimistic beliefs would probably come an inability to undertake reasoning that conforms to the standards of logic.

The pattern of distortion I have described is confirmed by case studies. In his book, *Wisdom, Madness and Folly*, John Custance describes with great clarity his affective disorders, diagnosed as manic–depressive reactions. His condition at its most extreme involved hallucination and thought disorder and, for reasons given earlier, we shall not concern ourselves with that aspect of his long episodes of mania and depression. He also experienced milder forms of elation and despair in which, as we shall see, his judgement was distorted by his condition in the way I have sketched earlier. He spent several months, he writes, '. . . in a state of elation which would probably be classified as mild hypomania, enjoying the marvels of the new world which had appeared to me and day-dreaming in the wildest manner of the future [before being] carried away in a disastrous but revealing climax which put an end to the manic period' (Custance, 1952, p. 47).

During the mild episode of mania thus described, he speaks of a lifting of a sense of guilt over his (real) sexual sins:

> I was sure of forgiveness. Moreover the meaning of my vision seemed to be that the love of the flesh and the love of the spirit, eros and agape, were really one, so that the impulses of sex were not sinful but rather the holy fount of life itself . . . the antagonism between sex and religion which is normal in Western Christianity, was turned into an alliance in my mind

and then he describes the course of action invited by this revelation:

> Religious feelings and emotions eventually combined with sexual impulses to cause me to give away some three hundred

> pounds, which I could ill afford, to ladies of easy virtue. . . .
> [In London] I was accosted . . . somewhere near Bond Street.
> It did not for a moment occur to me to pass on; I should have
> felt that to be a wicked action. It was a call. Somebody
> wanted me and I could not refuse. She was not in the least
> attractive but I felt that I loved her and wanted to help her.
> Strangely enough she had a Bible in her room, and we read it
> together. I gave her five pounds

It seemed to him that he had found a mission: he must serve these
women (Custance, 1952, p. 48):

> I gave money away until my bank warned me about my
> overdraft, but I was convinced that God would give me
> money to carry on the good work, and approached the
> Christian Science Church in Curzon Street with a request for
> money for a particular girl in whom I was interested. Very
> naturally they refused

He goes on to recount how, as his condition then worsened, he
indignantly retaliated for the church's perceived indifference and
was forcibly returned to a psychiatric institution.

What is telling for us in this account of his reasoning is not the
oddity of the ideas and feelings he experienced as such, but the
effect they had on his attitudes in particular – in this case, towards
money. He lost the ability to see that such extravagance was not
within his means and to predict future events in a reasonable way.
The optimistic and unrealistic thinking which allows that apparent problems will be resolved (with God's help, in this case), is
characteristic of the mood of elation that he experienced.

To characterize such moods of mania and depression without
acknowledging this cognitive aspect is to fail to give a full account
of them. As soon as this cognitive feature is allowed, we can see
how they might lead to distorted reasoning – for example, about
the future. Because he was in the grip of the unrealistic optimism
over money, Custance could not rationally assess the likelihood
of his remaining solvent.

Custance's distorted thinking may be compared with a second
case where thinking about the future appears again to be distorted
as the result of holding very general false beliefs. A writer,

described as subject to manic episodes, learned one day that a play of his had been bought by a film company (quoted in Sarason and Sarason, 1980, p. 248):

> He was in Florida when he got the news. He promptly bought himself a new Cadillac and some Chivas Regal and went tearing back to New York. On the way, he was picked up for speeding in a small town in Georgia and thrown into the clink. They allowed him one phone call, and whom did he call? He did not call me (his therapist); he did not call his wife; he did not even call his mistress. He called the Strategic Air Command to bomb the jail

As with Custance's unrealistic confidence in God's help, this man's optimistic plan reveals grave errors of judgement.

Like the parallel optimistic beliefs of mania, we can see how the pervasive despair of depression could affect reasoning about the future. Showing an equivalent concern over money to that of Custance in his distorted reasoning is the case of a wealthy, middle-aged man (Cameron, 1963, p. 522) who

> . . . was certain over a period of a year that he was penniless and would starve to death. His accountant and his banker brought him certified statements of his real financial situation; but he called the statements 'fakes', and he angrily tossed them aside. His lawyer also tried his hand at demonstrating the patient's financial solvency, but he finally gave up

A cognitive analysis of affective states like the one outlined here has been introduced in experimental studies. The central hypothesis of Beck's cognitive theory of depression (Beck, 1967, 1974, 1976, 1978) is that the depressed individual's negative view of the world, himself or herself and the future is not only present in but itself causes the accompanying feelings of despair and hopelessness. It is argued that 'overgeneralization, minimization of the positive and maximization of the negative' characterize the thinking of depressed people – traits which are illustrated in the following case (Beck, 1974, p. 10) when, after an argument with her brother, a mildly depressed woman concluded:

'I am incapable of being loved and of giving love,' and she felt
more depressed. . . . When a friend was too busy to chat with
her on the phone, she thought, 'She doesn't want to talk to
me any more.' If her husband came home late from the office,
she decided that he was staying away to avoid her. When her
children were ill-natured at dinner time, she thought, 'I have
failed them'

Whether or not the more radical causal hypothesis – that the
beliefs give rise to the feeling – holds, Beck's work and subsequent
experimental use of the Beck Depression Inventory seems to
confirm the notion that distorted cognitive states can be isolated
in depressed people. Because of the presence of parallel general
beliefs in hypomania, we can attribute defects of reasoning to the
hypomania sufferer as well.

Thus it seems correct to conclude that the pervasive despair and
elation of severe nonpsychotic depression contain general beliefs
likely to result in errors of judgement and distorted reasoning.
They can be shown to do so, moreover, in particular cases. And if
they do not? We can imagine at least the possibility of a person
whose extensive and intense despair or elation did not alter his or
her reasoning and whose general optimistic or pessimistic beliefs
were somehow strangely idle and did not enter into reasoning or
action. A similar case was suggested earlier when it was argued
that the cognitive elements of these moods are so central that,
were a person persistently to avow the feeling without in any way
giving evidence in reasoning or action of those general beliefs, we
would doubt the person's sincerity or self-knowledge.

However, such a case might be seen differently. It would be
possible for us to be convinced of the accuracy of the
phenomenological claim (convinced, that is, of its being real
despair) on account of some behavioural confirmation unrelated
to reasoning – lethargy and slowed speech, for example. Still, in
the absence of any impairment in reasoning, we would surely be
inclined to make the charge of a want of reason in such a case on
the basis of the major inconsistency between beliefs simultaneously entertained. If I believe, out of pervasive despair, an
excessively negative interpretation of future events and yet at the
same time my reasoning in no way reflects this belief but indicates
instead a more optimistic assessment, then – when the beliefs are

as general and far-reaching as they must be in such an extreme mood – a want of reason would (rightly) be ascribed to me.

In summary then, 'unreason' seems accurately to describe the characteristic pessimistic and optimistic beliefs and thought patterns shown to mark the states of pervasive depression and mania, respectively. Lesser traits of pessimism and optimism are also found in the sane person and thus are familiar to us from everyday life.

Notes

1 Thus it is said that the paranoid with jealous or erotic delusions is exquisitely sensitive to erotic feelings in others, while grandiose delusions grow out of the sensitivity to hostile feelings in others also grounding the more common persecutory delusions described here.
2 As well as a blunting and flattening of any emotional response.

8
Deviance and Defect

I have been arguing that our impulse to excuse the insane rests on various forms of unreason which they exhibit and I have taken pains to show that the sources of this unreason are particular defects of reasoning and judgement. Thus, while the insane are also distinguishable in many other respects – for instance, in having strange and unusual beliefs and desires – appeal to these other differences is not necessary to account for their exculpating want of reason. The kind of distinction adopted here, which I describe as that between defect and deviance, is one which is respected and deemed important by several philosophers concerned with normativism and madness (see Flew, 1975; Edwards, 1982). Such distinctions have not always been acknowledged, however.

Attacks on the Distinction

The narrow 'cognitivist' or 'intellectual' focus on madness adopted in this book has been criticised, implicitly and explicitly, in several contemporary discussions and requires further explanation and justification. First, it must be stressed that I am not offering a definition of madness as such in proposing an unreason analysis, but merely an account of what it is about madness which seems to exculpate when wrongdoing results from it. Thus I am unconcerned by a recent argument, for example, that mental aberration cannot be defined in cognitivist terms because of such conditions as masochism – the aberrant desire to harm oneself apparently unaccompanied by any cognitive defect (Culver and Gert, 1982). For a general account of madness it may be that unreason would prove an insufficient characterization and additional factors would need to be included. However, the issue of excuse does not enter into it when derangement is restricted to self

110

harm: the legal problem surrounding masochism concerns the Parens Patrie doctrine, not insanity as an excuse. The masochist requires protection from himself or herself, and no question of the action requiring a defence arises.

Secondly, I wish to deal with an attack on the cognitivist or intellectualistic approach which implies that the cost of maintaining it would be the sacrifice of certain linguistic and moral intuitions about the notion of irrationality. This is in Herbert Fingarette's discussion of exculpating irrationality in *The Meaning of Criminal Insanity* (1967).

Fingarette has explored the notion that what warrants our intuition to excuse the insane might best be characterized as irrationality. In this respect his work parallels mine quite closely. However, he has introduced a much broader notion of irrationality than the concept of unreason developed here, and one whose breadth, I shall argue, destroys the value of his thesis. Fingarette nowhere formally defines irrationality, but he offers the following characterization (p. 180):

> It is when 'rational' and 'irrational' pertain to conduct, to the practical, and when they can be used to characterise not only intellect but also the emotions, attitudes, desires and the person himself, that we have a use which is central to the concept of insanity

From the account quoted it is apparent that on Fingarette's interpretation of the notion of irrationality, the exculpating irrationality of the insane rests as much in their having extremely unusual or deviant desires, responses and beliefs as it does in their having unsound or defective judgement. He explicitly repudiates the position I am maintaining which he describes as the pervasive tendency in psychiatric and legal literature '. . . to slide from "rational" to "cognitive" as if they were equivalent' (p. 182, footnote). In order to get away, he says (p. 183), from

> the grave confusions inherent in reifying Reason, in thinking of the faculty of reason as a distinct and autonomous agency and one that is essentially the agency of the intellectual powers, we must emphasise the concept of rational conduct

Conduct, for Fingarette (1967, p. 183),

is insane, crazy, mad, irrational when it is not shaped in the
light of certain norms. These norms are not only norms of
correct inference or valid argument; they are norms regarding what emotions, or moods, or attitudes, or desires are in
some sense suitable or proper with respect to certain other
aspects of one's situation. Clearly there is much room for
variety here, for individuality and even idiosyncracy. But
there are limits

So being different, as much as demonstrating a want of reason, for
Fingarette counts as exculpating irrationality. 'Irrationality' pertains to infringements of norms for emotions, moods, attitudes
and desires as well as for reasoning.

Two sorts of consideration are introduced in support of the
position taken in these passages. First, there is an argument from
linguistic usage: Fingarette asserts that the terms 'rational' and
'irrational' are standardly used in the broader way he adopts
(p. 182). Secondly, there is an argument from our moral intuitions. He draws attention to the failure of knowledge tests for
criminal insanity like M'Naghten to capture all the kinds of
insanity which we would be inclined to suppose excusable.

In what follows, the narrower criterion for exculpating insanity
– rejected by Fingarette – will be defended. Each of his arguments
can, I think, be answered. Fingarette has too hastily dismissed the
norms of 'correct inference and valid arguments' in his search for
the basis of the different treatment due to the insane.

Let us look first at the linguistic argument. Because I have
chosen to speak of unreason rather than 'irrationality', and the
term 'unreason' suffers less from the broadly normative connotations which Fingarette discerns in the notion of irrationality,
my argument is technically safe from his challenge. However, I
shall respond to his argument as it concerns the notion of
irrationality insofar as to insist that, even given the facts of usage
he reports, respect for usage ought to be sacrificed in the light of
the dire theoretical consequences entailed in accepting the broader
notion of irrationality which he endorses. As to the second claim
concerning moral intuitions, I shall argue that extensions of the
cognitive criterion hitherto undeveloped, such as those discussed
in Chapter 7, can go far towards accommodating the breadth of
our intuition to excuse. I shall also argue that when deviance *alone*
is present the impulse for *different* treatment for the wrongdoer

must be distinguished from an impulse to excuse as such. The psychopathic personality, for example – whose condition is notably one of deviance without defect of judgement – is one which, while deserving different treatment from the ordinary wrongdoer, is not by dint of that to be judged to have an excuse. (This kind of case is discussed further at the end of the chapter.)

Fingarette's argument represents a challenge for my analysis because the distinction between deviance and defect cuts across the broad collection of responses which he describes as irrational. Departure from the norms of 'inference and valid argument' are defects of reasoning, to which exculpating irrationality – or unreason – is, in my view, correctly ascribed. However, deviations from other norms he describes – those concerned with emotions, moods and some attitudes and desires (this qualification will be discussed in a moment) – are deviance, on my account, and do not serve as such to exculpate.

I will now explain the two qualifications just mentioned. First, Fingarette has spoken loosely of attitudes and desires as if they were all of the same kind, but only some attitudes and desires need count as deviant. For both attitudes and desires are sometimes rationally – and hence sometimes nonrationally – based. They are formed through a reasoning process. I might establish an attitude on the basis of information obtained about a particular class – monkeys, for example. *Grounded* attitudes and desires of this kind correspond in every way to beliefs: departures from the norms of inference and validity in their formation count as defects of reasoning – not feeling – just as they do in the formation of beliefs. It is only those attitudes and desires which, like emotions, come unbidden without a cognitive process that are to be classified as deviant when they depart from what is normal; improperly formed grounded attitudes and desires are defects. When abhorrence of monkeys is unreasonable, it is so not on account of its unusual intensity or object but because, for instance, I formed it on the basis of poor inductive grounds. We have seen enough of the pervasive unreason of madness to expect that the severely disturbed person's grounded desires would show this defect.

The distinction between grounded and ungrounded attitudes and desires is an obvious one, but it deserves stress, for much of the plausibility of Fingarette's view depends on his failure to acknowledge it.

My second qualification concerns the role played by affective states in exculpating nonreason. The presence of unusual emotions, moods and ungrounded attitudes and desires do not, as such, signify a reason for exculpation, on my analysis. Nevertheless, as I have argued in Chapter 7, the presence of deviant affective states in conditions such as mania and depression standardly affects the formation of beliefs and grounded desires so that they depart from the norms of inference and valid reasoning. Thus while affective states of emotion and mood at least are not themselves defective, when they occur in affective disorders, they serve as indicators of the presence of defects of reasoning – and hence of exculpating unreason.

Let us look again at the broad collection of aberrant attributes which Fingarette wishes to include in the category of exculpating irrationality. Abnormal emotions and moods, as we have just seen, can be expected to result in defective reasoning. Desires and attitudes, moreover, may be ungrounded or grounded, so not all departures from normal desires and attitudes need concern us and those which are grounded will be subject to the classification of nonrationality in the same way that beliefs are when they depart from norms of reasoning. Finally, ungrounded attitudes – like persistent, unreasoned prejudices – seem to be made up of elements already dealt with. They combine emotions and moods – like the distaste I feel for the object of my attitude – together with desires – like the wish to avoid it.

Only the category of aberrant, ungrounded desires remains from the long list of aberrations with which we began and which Fingarette finds unaccounted for in the narrow, 'cognitivist' analysis of the kind he attacks. While Fingarette, as we have seen, lists the entire, rather inflated, set of attributes when describing aberrations fitting his broad notion of irrationality, it is in fact on a case of aberrant desires which his argument rests. In looking at the kinds of case which traditional cognitive tests of criminal insanity have failed to cover, he cites only one – the case of Fish. A 'completely habitual child killer and child eater' (Fingarette, 1967, p. 177), Fish was found sane under a traditional insanity test. Fingarette describes this man as a paradigm of insanity.

His emotional reactions and desires were in some respects so distorted that he had not the capacity to act rationally insofar as these came into play. However, his intellectual and perceptual capacities were not ever substantially impaired, nor was he, apparently, dominated by depressed or manic moods. When he ate children or stuck sharp objects into his body, he knew what he was doing, and he knew – as his actions showed – that what he was doing was contrary to law and public morality. He acted voluntarily, entirely on his own, and deliberately

Fish is portrayed as aberrant *only* in his desires (to kill and eat children and to hurt himself), which we may suppose to have been ungrounded. As such, his case is typical of one broad kind of condition which standardly fails to meet traditional tests for criminal insanity – that of sadism. (Fish was also masochistic, but the legal problem surrounding masochism, as I have indicated, does not concern insanity as a defence.)

Sadism, or sexual sadism, is sometimes classified as a character disorder or sexual dysfunction (American Psychiatric Association, 1980) rather than as a psychotic or neurotic illness as such, and this itself indicates something of its uneasy status. The condition has been defined clinically (Linde, 1976, p. 48) as,

a deviation characterised by torture or killing or mutilation of other persons in order to achieve sexual gratification

If it were true, as this description seems almost to hint, that the only sexual satisfaction available to the sadist was through this means, or even that it always resulted in consciously experienced sexual satisfaction, then there would be grounds for distinguishing sadism from ordinary cruelty. But the sexual gratification of the sadist, as other sources point out (American Psychiatric Association, 1980), may be unconscious. Moreover, it may not be his only form of sexual satisfaction. The line, then, between the sadist and a sane person subject to ordinary desires to inflict pain, which may also bring unconscious satisfaction, is uncomfortably thin. In choosing this condition to illustrate his position, Fingarette has revealed its weakness: the sufferer of disorders like Fish's sadism – or like the antisocial tendencies of the psychopathic or antisocial personality (to be discussed at more length presently) – lies on the border-line between sanity and madness where intuitions to excuse – as, indeed, an inclination to speak of pathology – fade out despite the repugnance and extreme nature of such cases. Sadists and psychopaths are puzzling cases, whose condition the law has consistently refused to regard as exculpating (Goldstein, 1967) and whose status as clinical conditions has been subject to dispute.

Legal hesitation in classifying character disorders as criminal insanity (and thus as exculpating conditions) seems to rest on the impulse to separate mad from bad. A condition characterized by nothing but aberrant desires to harm others cannot be adequately distinguished from sheer evil. There seems no way to separate the case of Fish, for example, from paradigmatic cases of wilful wickedness like that of Cesare Borgia described by Flew (1975, p. 93) in developing the distinction between the insane and the merely unusual, or deviant:

> The thirst for blood on its own account, the devilish delight in destruction . . . clearly exemplified in Borgia . . . whose crudities were certainly out of all proportion to the ends they had in view

History has judged Borgia to have been more bad than mad. While contemporary understanding may invite a description of pathology and a rewriting of history, the law cannot so readily relinquish exemplars of its fundamental categories. Jurisprudence requires that a distinction be maintained between those who are deranged – and so blameless – and those who wilfully and knowingly do wrong and deserve censure. Because the Borgias constitute not mere instances of the category but something by way of historical paradigms, to rewrite that historical judgement would be tantamount to casting doubt on the very dichotomy itself.

There are other conditions which Fingarette might have used to illustrate the broad sense of exculpating irrationality which he wishes to defend: affective disorder when unaccompanied by psychosis, and pure paranoia. While they seem at first to illustrate deviance of feeling and belief, respectively, in the absence of any defect of reasoning, on close examination these two conditions reveal such defects, as was shown in Chapter 7. The categories about which there is some agreement, and which might thus be thought to support his case, cannot be used to strengthen Fingarette's position, and the one to which he does appeal – Fish's sadism – is insufficiently central to establish his point.

To summarize then, about Fingarette's arguments for a broader notion of exculpating irrationality that includes deviance as well as defects of reason, we must conclude that if the linguistic intuition to which he attests is indeed present it must be sacrificed. The notion of nonrationality must be given a more restrictive connotation. Were we to respect his linguistic intuition, the cost – no way to distinguish the eccentric and unusual or the morally evil from the insane – would be too high.

Fingarette's claim that only the broader notion of irrationality can accommodate the breadth of our moral intuitions to excuse, moreover, may be challenged. For we have seen that the kinds of case upon which Fingarette's argument rests – the so-called character or personality disorders – are just those where the moral intuition to excuse breaks down. The strong sense that those suffering mental disorders are different enough from ordinary bad people *to be excused from blame* fails us in such cases.

Psychopathic Personality and Sexual Sadism

The conditions known as psychopathic personality and sexual sadism deserve further attention. This is partly because they are prominent among conditions whose status as psychiatric problems is questioned, but it is more than that. While not alone on the border-line between sane and clinically aberrant behaviour, the psychopath and the sadist deserve attention because of the frequency with which they are the perpetrators of serious offences against others. They are characterized by attitudes and desires which show a disregard or disrespect for other persons, as we shall see.

The characteristics of sadism, of which Fish's case seems not untypical, were introduced earlier. The clinical description fits Borgia – or any of the famous mass murderers or torturers of history. The sadist's desires and pleasures alone rather than any cognitive incapacity, seem to distinguish him or her from other people, and they are perhaps insufficient to separate him or her from some very wicked ones.

The puzzling category of psychopathic personality has long troubled thoughtful students of psychiatric nosology, and it is one which bears close parallels to the sadistic personality. Like the sadist, the psychopath is usually portrayed as sane except in having a set of desires and values at odds with that of the rest of the population.[1] He is presented as neither neurotic nor psychotic, as not in any way deranged or disordered in mind or behaviour but as incapable, in the words of a standard text (Clegley, 1950, pp. 380, 387), of

> . . . mature, wholehearted anger, true or consistent indignation, honest solid grief, sustained pride, deep joy, genuine despair . . . ordinary responsiveness to special consideration, kindness or trust

Using alternative nomenclature (Antisocial Personality), the American Psychiatric Association's DSM III describes (1980, p. 103)

> A lack of socialization alone with behaviour patterns that bring a person repeatedly into conflict with society; incapacity for significant loyalty to others or to social values; callousness; irresponsibility, impulsiveness, and inability to feel guilt or learn from experience or punishment. Frustration tolerance is low and such people tend to blame others or give plausible rationalization for their behaviour

Nineteenth-century psychiatry baldly acknowledged the moral element in these descriptions and classified the condition as the character disorder of 'moral imbecility' in order to distinguish these moral defects from the intellectual defects of more standard conditions. However, its modern names – 'psychopathic personality', then 'sociopathic personality' and, most recently, 'antisocial personality disorder' – were designed at least to stem the 'stigmatization' (Cameron, 1963) invited by the moralistic label, even if they could not alter the deeply moralistic tone of the clinical description.

Other conditions – masochism, for instance, or fetishism – share with psychopathic personality and sadism this feature of being characterized merely in terms of aberrant desires, attitudes and pleasures. However, psychopathic personality and sadism stand out in the peculiarly amoral quality of the relationship that their sufferers adopt to others. The sadist desires another's suffering; the psychopath is fundamentally indifferent to it. These are attitudes at odds with the most deep-seated notions of a shared morality.

We recognize a similarity with other nonclinical categories here, and with the response provoked by them. Our attitude towards a person committed to the moral position of egoism seems similar, or towards the fanatic of whom the moral philosopher Hare (1963) writes: a Nazi, or the Emperor Heliogabalus, who is said to have had people slaughtered for the sight of red blood on green grass. Such values and motivation are deeply opaque to us.

We are troubled in several ways by these cases of what might be called moral alienation (the sadist, the psychopath, the egoist, the fanatic). We struggle with their classification as sane. [Hare's response is to insist that such values as the fanatic's could not be truly adopted by anyone but a madman (1963, p. 172).] Anyone so different, it is often supposed, must be mad. We are puzzled, moreover, as to the appropriate treatment for them. They seem to deserve a punishment, but a different one – something to mark their failure to accept the notion of a common morality. Symbolically, it is *exile* – not prison – which captures what seem their just deserts.

The struggle to classify and then to appropriately punish such wrongdoers as these suggests that, were an adult not otherwise insane and yet sufficiently different, that very difference would warrant different treatment for wrongdoing. However, different treatment from that which is customary, does not have to be the same as the treatment meted out to the insane. Even if we resist the inclination to classify these kinds of moral alienation as psychiatric conditions, it remains true that for them ordinary punishment seems in some important way to miss the point.

In summary then, we do no violence to broadly agreed moral intuitions by limiting the class of the criminally insane whom we would excuse to those suffering clear defects of reason and not mere deviance. For most deviance – both that associated with cognitive and with affective states – is also defective: the states reflect unreason. When they do not – that is, when there are psychiatric conditions characterized solely by their deviance, like sadism and psychopathic personality – the intuition to judge them as excuses for wrongdoing seems also to be more equivocal and so less reliable as a guide to their treatment. Widespread agreement that the sufferer was not responsible is absent in these cases.

Note

1 Some descriptions of psychopathic personality hint at the presence of particular disabilities (for example, the inability to feel guilt) and not mere deviance; similarly, clinical descriptions sometimes seem to suggest that the sadist's desires are overpowering and compulsive in their quality. Were these characterizations standardly present and as amply and convincingly documented as they are in the other disorders we have been discussing, then we should indeed be required to consider psychopathy and sexual sadism as forms of disability rather than as mere deviance. However, the clinical literature is vague and inconsistent on these points and, despite the DSM III characterization quoted here, the overall picture of psychopaths and sadists portrays deviance rather than defect.

9

The Legal Tradition: Exculpating Ignorance and Compulsion

I wish now to explore the concept of an exculpating want of reason in the insane and in children. Two points about this issue are clear and indisputable. There is a widespread conviction that the insane and children require special treatment when they do wrong – that they are blameless or at least less culpable than ordinary sane adult criminals guilty of the same crime – and members of both groups are judged to be wanting in reason or rational capacity. Still we must explore the issue further for answers to other questions. Do children and the insane exhibit the same want of reason? Does this want of reason function as an excusing condition?

In showing that the same kinds of want of reason occur in children and in the insane and that they are exculpating, I hope to provide support for the principle of exculpating nonrationality itself. In the light of our parallel intuitions in both cases, the presence of a similar want of reason in the insane and in children would seem to confirm that the characteristic of unreason was itself an excusing condition. To establish this parallel between children and the insane I shall appeal to three separate consider-ations: first, legal support for the principle of exculpating unreason; secondly, the presence of moral intuitions to excuse juvenile offenders which seem to correspond in those we have concerning the insane; and, thirdly, the presence of forms of unreason in children which parallel the unreason of the insane.

Legal Formulations

Legal sources for the principle of exculpating nonrationality derive from the traditional treatment of both children and the

121

insane. First, there are formulations concerning the insane wrongdoer. These are relatively recent, dating no earlier than the last century in most instances, and the most important and central sources of these are cases where insanity was used as a defence.

Secondly, formulations are found in discussions on the status of child offenders. These, in contrast, arise earlier in the tradition. However, they are scant or nonexistent after the emergence of the Juvenile Court movement at the end of the nineteenth century which introduced separate courts for children.

The reasons for these historical disparities are interesting. The notion of insanity as an excuse for wrongdoing, as we have seen, was slow to emerge out of earlier conceptions in which contrary intuitions held sway. From the medieval understanding of the insane as deserving condemnation for their condition, to contemporary intuitions as to their blamelessness, was a shift so extreme, one might suppose, as to take place only gradually. Once recognized, however, the contemporary intuitions received increasing attention and refinement which has continued throughout the twentieth century.

The course of juvenile justice in the same period, in contrast, reflects new ways of perceiving children, and in contemporary discussions the issue of the moral guilt or innocence of the child is no longer raised. The child's innocence, it seems, is assumed rather than doubted – except where the presence of hard deterministic thinking renders the notion obsolete. It is side stepped however; emphasis is now laid on the possibility of helping and reforming juvenile offenders, and the question of the basis for our intuition that they are morally innocent has been forgotten. This point was made boldly by Mr Justice Fortas when he delivered the opinion of the US Supreme Court in the influential Gault case (*In Re Gault*, p. 1026) and spoke of a philosophy underlying the whole Juvenile Court movement. Appalled by adult penalties and procedures, he said, the early reformers were convinced that

> . . . society's duty to the child could not be confined by the concept of justice alone. [They believed that] society's role was not to ascertain whether the child was 'guilty' or 'innocent' but 'what is he, how has he become what he is, and what had best be done in his interest and in the interest of the state to save him from a downward career'.

At least in its pronouncements, juvenile law today completely reflects this philosophy. The question of the child's moral guilt or innocence, and hence the notion of excuses, does not arise. Nevertheless, despite this historical disparity between the sources from which legal formulations of the principle of exculpating nonrationality derive, we shall see that it is the same principle in each sphere.

The Principle of Exculpating Nonrationality

While the law seems to point to a principle of an exculpating nonrationality, it is to be criticized both for the narrow formulations it has offered of the defects of reason in question and for the narrow interpretation those formulations have received, each of which has failed to account for the breadth of the moral intuitions involved. What is required then is the development of a fuller account of the nonreason which exculpates – a task which I shall complete in the final chapter. In this chapter, two issues will be separated and treated in turn: references to the principle of exculpating nonrationality in juvenile and insanity law and references to the particular defects of reason or judgement supposed to comprise that want of reason with which the principle is concerned.

We find the principle unequivocally stated in law pertaining to the insane and to children. Both in earlier references preceding the regular use of the insanity plea (such as that quoted in Chapter 1) and in discussions of insanity as a defence, appeal is made to a failure of mental capacity or a defect of reason on the part of the insane criminal as the ground for exculpation. Moreover, the exculpation of child offenders rests squarely upon appeal to the notion of their want of reason. The shared principle is nicely revealed in the following statement from the fourteenth century (quoted in Sanders, 1970, p. 11):

> It is not Burglary in an Infant of fourteen years of age . . . nor in natural fooles, or other person that bee *non compos mentis*
> . . .

Here children, the insane and retarded[1] (natural fooles), or anyone else lacking control of his or her mind (*compos mentis*) are explicitly linked.

In common law, children are conclusively presumed not to have the mental capacity to commit crime until 7 years of age, while between 7 and 14 years of age they are treated as having a rebuttable presumption of no such capacity which must be overcome by the prosecution before guilt can be found. Moreover, as Blackstone points out, it has not been chronological age as such which determines culpability in juvenile cases but rather the strength of the delinquent's *understanding* and *judgement* (my emphasis), 'since one lad of eleven years may have as much cunning as another of fourteen' (Blackstone, 1765–67, p. 432).

The principle, then, is evident, but to what defects of understanding and judgement does it refer?

Kinds of Exculpating Nonrationality

The young child and the insane person may be said to lack reason in many obvious ways, some similar and some different, which result in their needing special care and treatment, for example, and in their being less reliable in certain respects than sane adults. We can suppose that the reference to 'defects' of reason, in this recurrent phrase, points to such obvious incapacities. This point seems most evident in juvenile law where the expressions 'lacking reason', 'lacking understanding', 'lacking discretion' and the notion of not being in control of one's mind (*non compos mentis*), all occur frequently and apparently interchangeably – and seem to indicate a general incapacity or a set of incapacities, rather than any particular one.

In addition, however, reference is made in the earlier legal tradition to one particular failure or incapacity. The child and the insane criminal alike are said to lack criminal intent or malice and are therefore not to be punishable for their wrongs.

The notion of criminal intent or *mens rea* (the guilty mind) is an important one in early legal thinking and it is always entwined with a certain concept of knowledge – knowledge, particularly, of the wrongfulness of what was done or knowledge, as it is often put, of wrong from right. Thus a central part of establishing the moral innocence of children, when this task was undertaken, used to involve showing that they were *doli incapax*, and could not discern between good and evil. Blackstone (1765–67, pp. 432–3), for example, says,

> . . . under fourteen, though an infant shall be *prima facie* innocent and judged to be *doli incapax*, yet if it appear to the court and jury that he was *doli capax*, and could discern between good and evil, he may be convicted and suffer death

Insanity Law: Knowledge Tests

The notion that exculpating nonrationality resides in certain kinds of ignorance is also the burden of the first and most influential test for criminal insanity – M'Naghten's Rule. Formulated in England in 1843 after the case of a deranged political assassin, Daniel M'Naghten, who shot Drummond under the (justified) misapprehension that he was the Tory Prime Minister Sir Robert Peel, the rule (*Daniel M'Naghten's Case*) states that to establish a defence on the ground of insanity,

> . . . it must be clearly proved that, at the time of the committing of the act, the party accused was labouring under such a defect of reason, from disease or defect of the mind, as not to know the nature and quality of the act he was doing; or if he did know it, *that he did not know that what he was doing was wrong* [my emphasis]

The knowledge criterion in M'Naghten goes beyond the moral knowledge of *doli capax*; knowing the nature and quality of an act covers more than merely knowing its wrongfulness. We shall return to the extended scope provided by this formulation presently. Nevertheless, the kind of moral knowledge we saw in parallel discussions of juvenile law is clearly intended here as well.

M'Naghten's Rule, moreover, merely formalized the moral knowledge criterion found in a long tradition concerning insanity. It is a tradition reaching back at least as far as Lambard's sixteenth-century *Eirenarcha*, introduced earlier, where it is stated 'that if a man or child y apparently hath *no knowledge of good or evil*, do kil a ma' [my emphasis], then this is no fellony, for they lack an understanding wil' (Lambard, 1581).

Thus a form of ignorance is the particular defect of reason indicated in the law to account for the *non compos mentis* state of the child and the mad person alike. And while the implicit force of expressions like 'defect of understanding' and 'lack of discretion' seems to be to convey exculpating nonrationality as comprising a broader range of defects, the law is silent on what precisely might be included.

The limitations of attributing an exculpating want of reason solely on the basis of the particular kind of ignorance we have been discussing are evident. They have been amply exposed and explored, as we shall see, in the insanity law following M'Naghten's case. And the neglect of the principle of exculpating nonrationality in recent juvenile law can alone account for the absence of a similar critique there. We will now look at the inadequacies of a narrow interpretation of this principle in each area.

M'Naghten's Rule is vulnerable to several criticisms, some of which have been anticipated by its detractors and amply developed in the extensive attack to which it has been subject almost since its first formulation. However, its critics have often obscured the real strengths of this rule by failing to distinguish the narrow and limited interpretation which it has received in law from the broader reading it would permit.

Difficulties in the rule may be classed into two categories: particular problems arising out of ambiguities in its terminology on the one hand and a general narrowness of focus which seems to preclude certain types of derangement altogether on the other.

First, let us look at the difficulties concerning particular words and phrases. The word 'know' in the key notions of knowing the act's wrongfulness and knowing its nature and quality may mean something as superficial as 'can assent to' ('intellectual knowledge', as it is often described by critics from psychiatry), and as deep as 'fully appreciate', and the fate of sufferers of several psychiatric disorders might rest on the choice of interpretation. A schizophrenic, for example, as has been pointed out, may be able to describe his action and its wrongfulness without being able to 'evaluate his conduct in terms of its actual impact upon himself and others [and] appreciate the total setting in which he acted' (Goldstein, 1967). On a narrow interpretation of 'know' this person's insanity could not be established.

Another consequence of such ambiguities is that there must be expected variation from trial to trial, depending on the reading of these phrases. Thus one central purpose of M'Naghten – to offer an equitable and standardized test – is lost.

The word 'wrong' is ambiguous also. There is a narrow interpretation, adopted in English courts, by which 'wrong' is understood as illegal, or contrary to the laws of the land, as the M'Naghten judges put it. In addition, wrong may be interpreted to read 'morally wrong', as has been pointed out, either in the sense of contrary to a personal code or in the quite different sense of contrary to the generally agreed upon standards of the community. A person might judge his or her action as wrong by the standards of others and yet as morally obligatory by the dictates of personal conscience – as do those practising civil disobedience. On one reading of 'wrong' this person knew that what he or she did was wrong; on another reading he or she did not. An acquittal by reason of insanity might again rest on the choice of interpretation.

Attempts have been made to substitute the unsatisfactory 'know' with broader terms like 'appreciate' (for example, the American Law Institute's *Model Penal Code*, 1955), although to do so is perhaps unnecessary. As a matter of historical fact, 'know' has usually been given a very narrow interpretation and restricted to an 'intellectual' awareness – from which its critics have falsely concluded that the difficulty resides in the term itself – but 'know' is open to a broader understanding. Indeed, in cases where courts have explicitly discussed the term's ambiguity and provided a reading, a broad construction has been favoured (Goldstein, 1973). Some of the recalcitrant cases, where our intuition to excuse extends beyond the condition captured by the test, could be dealt with merely by adopting a broader interpretation in this way – for example, that of the schizophrenic described earlier who, while able to say what he did, could not be said in some deeper sense to know it fully. This is not a difficulty intrinsic to M'Naghten but merely to the interpretation it has received in the law.

Alternatively, further breadth can be derived from the notion of knowing *the nature and quality* of the action. As an historical fact the 'nature and quality' phrase has been neglected, and various glosses on it have not substantially altered or extended its import (*Hoover* v. *State*; *McCune* v. *State*; *Regina* v. *Townley*; *People* v. *Pico*). It has been understood to refer merely to the act's physical nature or quality on the one hand or to its moral quality (its rightness or wrongfulness) on the other. Because of these restricted readings, it has been taken to advance little beyond the notion of knowledge of the act's wrongfulness (Goldstein, 1973), since knowing an act's moral nature seems to presuppose knowing its physical one.

Introducing a broader interpretation of the notion of knowledge of the nature and quality of an act enables us to explain our wish to extend exculpation to cases which seem recalcitrant both to the narrower interpretation of that idea and to the moral knowledge criterion. Suffering from either of several fairly standard kinds of disorder, a person might hold one of the following beliefs about the nature and quality of his or her action:

Case 1   Under the spell of persecutory beliefs not themselves grounded on hallucinatory experience a man might understand his act of assassination as justified self-defence (see *Daniel M'Naghten's Case*)

Case 2   Responding to the demands of hallucinated instructions from God, a man might regard his violence to his wife as an act of necessary obedience (see *People* v. *Schmidt*)

With a narrow interpretation of the phrase 'knowing the nature and quality', these beliefs would be compatible with such knowledge: in each case it could be said that the person knew the nature and quality of the action and thus should not be judged as criminally insane and excusable. Indeed, it might be argued that if each of these actions were not recognized as the kind it was (violent and destructive of another) it could not be seen as self-defence, and as obeying divine commands, respectively. Broadening the notion of knowing the nature and quality of the action enables us to treat these cases differently. There was error and ignorance involved in Daniel M'Naghten's belief that the Tories intended to harm him, as there was in the belief of the defendant in the Schmidt case (*People* v. *Schmidt*) that he must attack his wife to obey divine instructions. According to a common epistemological formulation by which knowledge requires true, justified belief, it is clear that the beliefs in *Cases 1* and 2 – which are neither true nor justified – are not knowledge.

The fact of the immediate act of violence may be known and understood without confusion and its wrongfulness entirely appreciated but still its perpetrator may suffer exculpating ignorance concerning it. By interpreting the 'nature and quality' phrase broadly, a knowledge test like M'Naghten can be shown to accommodate this point.

One difficulty might be thought to arise with these broader interpretations of M'Naghten. If knowledge refers to a deep understanding and appreciation of the nature and quality of the act, then many sane wrongdoers must also be judged ignorant of their actions. The M'Naghten formulation allows us to distinguish (theoretically, at least) between the exculpating ignorance of the insane and an everyday want of knowledge found in the sane: the former not merely exemplifies but stems from or is caused by a 'disease or defect' of the mind, while the latter does not. Only if the specific ignorance were understood to exemplify a general tendency and nothing more, so that the 'disease or defect' phrase merely referred to a disposition towards such ignorance, would the difficulty described be genuine; and there is no reason to suppose it need be – or was by its authors – so intended. The disease or defect of the mind may be taken to refer to an underlying state or condition providing a causal explanation of the particular lapse.

Yet even expanded in the ways I have suggested, knowledge tests of this kind are still insufficient to capture all the kinds of madness commonly judged to excuse and, as we shall see, appeal must be made to exculpating unreason as a separate excusing condition.

Insanity Law: Control Tests

In addition to difficulties stemming from the terminology of M'Naghten's Rule, it has been long recognized that there are certain sorts of disturbance marked more by a disparity of some kind between thought and behaviour than by faulty reasoning – volitional disorders, as they have been called. Being assailed by an overwhelming impulse to act when that action runs counter to all one's wishes and intentions is a problem of self control which is the sole characteristic of certain disorders. Because these disorders are not in general as severe as those marked by errors of judgement, and are thus not the object of the widespread and reliable intuition to excuse which I am taking to define the kinds of madness to be dealt with here, they are of less importance to my thesis. However, something must be said about the control tests, adopted to accommodate them, because of the role these tests have played in both marking out weaknesses and determining interpretation of knowledge tests.

The emphasis on loss of control, rather than on ignorance, has been raised as a counter to what has been judged the overly rationalistic quality of knowledge tests like M'Naghten's. In a long tradition which underwent revival in the 1920s with perceived support from the new 'depth psychology', it was proposed that the person accused should be classed as insane if his or her deed resulted from diminished self-control, and several additional tests for criminal insanity and additional qualifications have been adopted which make reference to the absence of self-control.

There have been varying constructions. Emphasis was placed on the person's *power to choose* between right and wrong in the influential early Parsons case, where the jury was required to decide 'if the disease of insanity can so affect the mind as to subvert the freedom of the will, and thereby destroy the power of the victim *to choose* between the right and the wrong, though he perceive it' (*Parsons* v. *State*). The *Davis* case refers to the will of the accused (defined as the governing power of the mind) as 'otherwise than voluntarily so completely destroyed that his actions are not subject to it, but are beyond his control' (*Davis* v. *State*). In other cases, emphasis has been on the inability to resist doing wrong (*Lee* v. *State*). Finally, the notion of an irresistible impulse was introduced in *Commonwealth* v. *Rogers* where the mind and will of the accused were said to be governed by 'an uncontrollable and irresistible impulse produced and growing out of mental disease'.

These formulations hint at differing models of will and self-control which are not insignificant, but ostensibly each appeals to the notion of *compulsion* – the second condition which serves to excuse in Aristotle's discussion, and a factor long recognized as providing an excuse in other areas of law.

Of those things which are thought involuntary, and thus not appropriate subjects for blame or praise, Aristotle (*Nichomachean Ethics*, 110a) says, (they) take place under compulsion (or owing to ignorance); and that is compulsory of which the moving principle is outside, being a principle in which nothing is contributed by the person who is acting or is feeling the passion, e.g. if he were to be carried somewhere by a wind, or by men who had him in their power (my parentheses added)

Aristotle's discussion is confusing because he raises doubts about the appropriateness of withholding blame from some of the kinds of coercion and duress which are usually treated as warranting excuse and lessened blame in moral and legal situations – for example, things done to avoid greater evil, like the case of the sea captain abandoning his cargo in a storm. These 'mixed actions', Aristotle points out, are in part voluntary (they are compelled but not forced). A more immediate difficulty is that the legal formulations quoted earlier seem to invoke the concept of behaviour which is *compulsive* rather than compelled. (Aristotle does insist that the insane are beyond the limits of virtue and vice (*Nichomachean Ethics*, 1148b 19–31, 1149b, 22–1150a5) but does not refer to them in this discussion.)

The concept of compulsion is also extremely problematical. There has been a long legal history of doubts and concerns about the parallel between the ordinary legal cases in which being compelled to act (due to duress, for example) counts as an excuse – sometimes called situational or environmental compulsion (Low, Jeffries and Bonnie, 1982) – and the special case of the mentally disturbed person acting compulsively. (The nineteenth-century jurist Stephen, for example, remarks that there are but three forms of compulsion: (1) compulsion of a husband over a wife; (2) compulsion by threats of injury to a person or property; and (3) compulsion by necessity. He adds, 'some forms of madness have some resemblance to compulsion, though I think the resemblance is superficial' (Stephen, 1883, p. 105).

In contemporary times it has been argued that compulsive action is not to be treated as analogous to action which is compelled, and the force of the disanology has often been taken to rest on Aristotle's criterion for compulsion: no external force necessitates the action of the person who acts compulsively. Introducing the notion of volitional disabilities, Culver and Gert (1982, p. 116) classify action which is compelled as *unfree* but *voluntary*, on the grounds that there are 'coercive incentives' without which the action would not have occurred. They argue that compulsive behaviour, in contrast, is not only unfree but *unvoluntary* (though intentional), because it is 'caused by something about the agent himself' namely, what they call a volitional disability. They decry the use of the term 'compulsion' by which voluntary and free actions are not distinguished because

> it leads one to regard 'inner compulsion' as identical to external compulsion, such as coercion, in all respects except that it comes from within the person rather than from without

These authors then go on to explain the non-voluntary character of the compulsive hand-washer's action,

> He knows what he is doing and wills to do it. However he does not do so voluntarily. He lacks the volitional ability to will to wash his hands. This paradoxical situation, of willing what one does not have the volitional ability to will, arises because having the *volitional ability to do X includes as a necessary feature willing not to do X in appropriate circumstances*. The volitional ability to will to do X requires that one can will not to do X. A compulsive hand washer wills to wash his hands, but since he cannot will not to wash his hands, he lacks the volitional ability to will to wash his hands [emphasis added]

Thus compulsive hand-washing reveals a 'volitional disability'.

Compulsion, we saw, has traditionally been regarded as an excusing condition. However, if acting compulsively is to be distinguished from being compelled to act, we cannot assume that the person who acts compulsively, or suffers a volitional disability in Culver and Gert's terminology, has an excuse for wrongdoing.

The so-called compulsive neurosis of the hand-washer, described earlier, where this kind of disability most frequently appears, is not associated with antisocial behaviour. But the question arises of whether compulsive action excuses with one particular condition: kleptomania, or compulsive stealing. (We are interested here in disorders characterized solely or primarily by compulsive behaviour. Compulsions may also occur as part of more severe disturbances, but then they are accompanied by other manifestations such as hallucination and thought disorder, and the question of exculpation *solely on the basis of compulsion* does not arise.) Stress on the distinction between compulsive action and that which is compelled has sometimes been introduced in support of the view that kleptomania is not, or should not be, a legal excuse. However, like Culver and Gert who regard the presence of volitional disabilities as a distinct ground for exculpation, I want to suggest that the sufferer from severe kleptomania has some measure of excuse because of his or her condition.

We must look more closely at this issue. The expression 'irresistible impulse' has often been used to describe the compulsion of the kleptomaniac. It suggests that we must view the compulsive as at the mercy of a stronger desire (to steal) than that of the ordinary thief who also steals or the law-abiding citizen who does not. However, the strength of a desire is distinguishable from its controllability (Shope, 1967) and we may also, and perhaps more helpfully, view compulsion as a breakdown or failure of certain abilities which are enjoyed by the sane person. It is not that the kleptomaniac's desire is stronger but that his or her ability to control or inhibit it is defective. The kleptomaniac cannot will not to steal in appropriate circumstances. Because to act compulsively is to demonstrate a particular disability in this way and is to manifest a kind of unreason (specifically, a failure to act for reasons), I am inclined to suppose that the severely compulsive behaviour of the kleptomaniac may be excusable, and counts as a form of exculpating unreason.

One last point remains to be considered here. The case of a defendant acting on hallucinated commands from God believed to have been issued on pain of death (see *People* v. *Schmidt*), bears some parallels to the sane wrongdoer subject to coercion. It is tempting to see both deeds of wrongdoing as *compelled* (though neither wrongdoer acts compulsively) and to appeal to the element of compulsion in explaining our impulse to excuse the wrongdoer in each case. Thus it may be supposed that in failing to include this way in which insanity may lead to compulsion and in devoting themselves to the notion of acting compulsively, control tests for insanity are wanting.

However, the crime of the psychotic who obeyed hallucinated divine commands is also importantly different from that of the sane wrongdoer coerced to act. The threat in the latter case is genuine and external while in the former one it is spurious and subjective. Our impulse to excuse the psychotic lies with his or her unavoidable error of judgement and, while he or she may be said to have been *obliged* to act, it will not be accurate to describe him or her as compelled to do so.

A separate problem with control tests lies in their application: establishing whether or not a person acted compulsively may be very difficult indeed (see *State* v. *Bundy*). As with M'Naghten and the knowledge tests derived from it, the various control tests also present difficulties at two levels. They contain ambiguous and confusing terminology: 'control', 'impulse', 'irresistible', and so on, are open to a number of different interpretations which make their application problematical and arbitrary, and they fail to include certain kinds of derangement. Many seriously deranged people have no problems with volition: what they want to do may be strange but the relationship between their desire and subsequent intentional action is not.

In order to accommodate the latter problem, attempts have been made to combine the cognitive and control tests. In several influential formulations, compulsion and ignorance (in the narrow interpretation which M'Naghten's wording has received) are treated as separately sufficient conditions for the ascription of exculpating insanity. [See the British Royal Commission on Capital Punishment (1953) and the American Law Institute's *Model Penal Code* (1955).] However, this too, while it helped in explaining the impulse to exonerate the sufferers of certain particular conditions like kleptomania, proved insufficient to capture all those we regard as severely disturbed. One may suffer a severe and exculpating derangement and yet have sufficient knowledge and control to pass any combination of the traditional tests for ignorance and compulsion – a point noted explicitly in *US* v. *Brawner* (p. 976):

> We felt the language of the old right/wrong/irresistible impulse rule for insanity was antiquated, no longer reflecting the community's judgement as to who ought to be held criminally liable for socially destructive acts

In several influential discussions of the control tests, the affective disorder of depression (or melancholia) – characterized by brooding and reflection – has been singled out as a notable instance of a severe disorder whose sufferer would be captured neither by control nor by knowledge tests (see *Durham* v. *US*). Another such case would seem to be pure paranoia. A person suffering from a severe but nonpsychotic depression or from some of the more sophisticated and seemingly reasonable delusions of pure paranoia, as we saw earlier, may not be guilty of any obvious false beliefs or faulty reasoning. Not only is that person not compelled to act, he or she is not ignorant – either in the narrow sense or even in the broader ways sketched earlier in this chapter. While it is not possible to capture the sufferers of these two conditions in traditional knowledge and/or control formulations, however, elements of *unreason* may be found in the judgement and thought processes of each, as was shown in Chapter 7. Because of this, a test for criminal insanity will be proposed in Chapter 11 which by-passes reference to the traditional notions of knowledge and control in favour of the broader notion of unreason. Like ignorance, unreason also occurs in the sane as well as in the insane. However, because we are dealing with a general incapacity, there will be no difficulty again – at least at a theoretical level – in distinguishing the trait which exculpates from that which does not, even though the notion of unreason is limited to the manifestations rather than the underlying states of madness. Features of the unreason itself distinguish the insane from the sane thinker. Due to the pervasiveness of the insane person's defects of reasoning, and the nature of his or her impulsiveness in the case of kleptomania, that person is robbed of the ability to avoid errors of judgement and action.

The failure of traditional excusing conditions to capture fully the unreason of madness is reflected in more recent formulations appealing frankly and exclusively to the *pathological* nature of insanity. The criminally insane are to be excused because they suffer a mental disease in formulations like the Durham Rule (*Durham* v. *U.S.*), for instance, which will be discussed more fully in Chapter 11. However, as was argued in Chapter 3, it does not seem that we can appeal to diseases as such to excuse wrongdoing. Such a formulation, rather than advancing the situation, seems to leave us without adequate grounds or justification for the impulse to excuse the insane.

The difficulties with traditional tests discussed here point to the insufficiency of narrow ignorance and compulsion criteria for an exculpating want of reason as it applies to the insane. Similar limitations emerge, we shall now see, when the child's exculpating want of reason is interpreted in this way.

Juvenile Law

In suggesting that we ground an impulse to excuse the child in one particular defect of reason or understanding, juvenile law also fails to go far enough. For neither particular ignorance of the kind understood in the concept of the guilty mind nor, indeed, that other traditional excusing condition, compulsion, entirely captures the kind of prerationality grounding an impulse to exonerate children.

Very young children would be ignorant of what they do in the narrow way embodied in the concept of the guilty mind, it is true; but older children offer fewer grounds for attributing a simple ignorance of right and wrong. The inability to make that moral distinction is certainly sufficient, when it is present, to ground our impulse to exculpate. The difficulty is that with older children this would not be present – yet the impulse to exonerate remains.

Early law rightly recognized that the notion of an exculpating want of reason to which it appealed would allow many children over 7 years of age to be fully culpable, and it is with approval that Blackstone (1765–7, p. 433) cites the case of an 8-year old boy who set fire to two barns. When tried he appeared to have

> malice, revenge and cunning [and] he was found guilty, condemned and hanged accordingly

Our impulse today is to suppose, surely, that however fully the child may have satisfied the court that he possessed malicious intent and cunning, he should not have been so judged. In some broader sense, we want to insist, he must have lacked an understanding of what he did.

The knowledge criterion for an exculpating want of reason in children may be extended to reflect M'Naghten's formulation. Adding ignorance of the nature and quality of the act to ignorance of its wrongfulness, will be helpful in certain cases. It may be sufficient, for example, to explain the ignorance of the boy described who, while he understood his action in some superficial sense, could hardly have fully appreciated its consequences and significance at 8 years of age. However, this extension will not completely capture the exculpating prerationality of children any more than it did, as we saw, that of the insane.

The older child who commits a crime may in some very general sense be ignorant, but it is not exactly an ignorance of the wrongfulness, nature or quality of any particular action, as I will now try to illustrate.

Let us consider again the cases where our intuition to exonerate seems to conflict with Blackstone's harsher standard. He introduces three cases, a 13-year-old girl who killed her mistress and two younger boys each guilty of murder, arguing that in the presence of their demonstrated ability to discern good from evil, each one was rightly subject to capital punishment.

The period between ages 7 and 14, he admits (p. 93) in introducing this discussion, is subject to much uncertainty,

> . . . for the infant shall, generally speaking, be judged *prima facie innocent;*

Nevertheless,

> . . . if he was *doli capax*, and could discern between good and evil at the time of the offence committed, he may be convicted and undergo judgement and execution of death, though he hath not attained to years of puberty or discretion. And Sir Matthew Hale gives us two instances one of a girl of thirteen, who was burned for killing her mistress; another of a boy still younger, that had killed his companion, and hid himself, who was hanged; for it appeared by his hiding that he knew he had done wrong, and could discern between good and evil; and in such cases the maxim of law is that *malitia supplet aetatem*. So also, in much more modern times, a boy of ten years old, who was guilty of a heinous murder, was held a proper subject for capital punishment by the opinion of all the judges

These children did act knowingly, in certain ways, as Blackstone insists. However, to treat the child's having hidden after his act of wrongdoing as demonstration of the same understanding and reason which having the sense to hide might show in a sane adult wrongdoer seems to be to ignore salient differences between children and adults. The child's hiding would be compatible with a total failure to comprehend the enormity and significance of the crime and its consequences; it would as likely have reflected an impulse or a resort to fantasy as it would a reasoned response. Nor is the child committing a crime exactly driven or compelled. It is true that he or she has not yet acquired the full capacity to choose and act enjoyed by adults, but to say that seems rather to introduce a new category to stand alongside the duality of freedom and compulsion than to say that the child was compelled to act. In Chapter 10 we shall see that the preconditions of what we suppose in an adult to be voluntary and deliberate action are a complex and interrelated set of cognitive and affective capacities which are fully acquired only at the end of childhood.

In summary then, appeal to something like a principle of exculpating nonrationality is evident in the legal tradition although it is not put in exactly that way. However, the law fails to provide an account of that nonrationality broad enough to meet the demands of the moral intuition reflected in that principle. A want of reason which exculpates must include more than the specific kind of ignorance characterizing the guilty mind, or that formulated in M'Naghten's Rule – even taken together with the compulsion referred to in the 'control' qualification. Though there are suggestions of a broader interpretation than either of these to be found in references to exculpating nonrationality in early juvenile law, because of contemporary neglect of that aspect of legal thinking, these remain insufficiently developed to be of use to us here.

In order to justify and ground the extent of our impulse to excuse the insane we need to appeal to a concept of the want of reason which exculpates fuller than that found in the Anglo–American legal tradition with its reference to the specific excusing conditions of ignorance and compulsion. Thus I shall propose that exculpating unreason be adopted as an additional excusing condition to stand alongside ignorance and compulsion.

Note

1 Although retardation is not an issue with which I shall deal, what is claimed here for children would appear to apply equally to those adults who are child*like* in the appropriate respects due to mental retardation.

10

Exculpating Unreason in Children

The notion of exculpating unreason derives from my earlier discussion of the manifestations of madness, but we must also look now at the ways in which children are wanting in reason. By examining the thought and action of children we can better understand the notion of exculpating unreason required for grounding our impulse to excuse. Moreover, by exploring the parallels which hold between the want of reason found in the insane and that found in children, we can derive support for the application of the principle of exculpating unreason in the case of the one by appeal to its presence in that of the other.

The scope of my analysis must first be clarified. I shall argue that only by appeal to their prerationality can a complete justification be found for our impulse to exonerate children. Yet there are also areas where our intuitions desert us and agreement ceases to be widespread. At what stage should we cease to appeal to the notion of childhood innocence to protect the juvenile offender from blame? How much reason and judgement must he or she exhibit?

The variety of answers offered to this question and the extent of the problem it raises are reflected in state-by-state variation in minimum ages for criminal responsibility throughout the United States, where differences can be as great as 5 years, depending on the crime (James, 1960). However, it is a problem for any theory of excuses – it is just as difficult for one who would argue that the insane should be excused from wrongdoing. That topic will not be discussed here: I do not pretend to know a manner of determining exactly where insanity gives way to sanity and full culpability should prevail, nor do I have an answer to the question when it is asked about children.

Prerational Thought in the Child

The child's lack of reason differs notably from that of the insane in one way: the child never has had the capacity to reason and yet, presumably, will one day acquire it. A want of reason in children reflects a normal development stage.

It is perhaps due partly to this important difference that, while the child is less than rational, the terms 'irrational' and 'unreasonable' seem to apply to the behaviour of children less naturally even than to that of the insane. In their effects on functioning, the child's and the mad person's lack of reason are analogous. Still, the term 'prerational' seems more appropriate in the child's case, indicating as it does the special developmental nature of the condition.

In considering prerational thought we may appeal to the careful studies of development psychology. Of these I shall concentrate on the writing of Piaget (1948, 1953, 1967) whose early investigations into children's thinking have not been disconfirmed by more recent findings (see Rosen, 1980; Windmiller, Lambert and Turiel, 1980). Piaget (1967, p. 77) has described broad stages in which the development of intelligence may be understood, and has explored the question of the child's moral and affective development, which he sees as intimately connected with it. As he puts it, his studies show

> what the young child lacks in order to be able to reason like an average middle-class adult

I shall outline Piaget's findings and then consider the way in which they illuminate our quest for a fuller account of the child's exculpating want of reason. However, it is less for the details of Piaget's interpretations of his observations, some of which may be questioned, than for certain broad conclusions to be drawn from them that I wish to focus on his work. First, Piaget's findings suggest that there is an interdependence between affective development (which includes what is usually called moral development) and intellectual development. Thus a child's having reached a point in moral development – that, let us say, at which moral responsibility could be ascribed for a certain class of actions – would require that a certain level of intellectual development had occurred. Without recognition of the distinction between his or her own and another's point of view (a stage of intellectual development), for example, Piaget found the child incapable of deliberate action (a stage in moral development).

Secondly, his observations show that intellectual development occurs very slowly, which suggests that the child is a teenager before he or she acts, reasons and communicates, in many significant respects, in the same way as sane adults.

Piaget's Analysis

Piaget distinguishes four stages of the child's intellectual and affective development of interest to us here: the intellectual revolution of the first two years, the Pre-operational thought of the child from ages 2 to 7, the development of Concrete Operations between ages 7 and 14 and, finally, the adolescent's acquisition of Formal Operations.

Consider first the preverbal sensorimotor stage. Initial *decentring* brings recognition that the physical self is a distinguishable from an external world. Only after a kind of miniature Copernican revolution, says Piaget, 'space finally becomes a general place that contains all objects including the child's own body' (Piaget, 1967, p. 79). At first, the infant's consciousness is entirely *egocentric* because 'there is no definite differentiation between the self and the external world' (Piaget, 1967, p. 12–13):

. . . the progress of sensorimotor intelligence leads to the construction of an objective universe in which the subject's own body is an element amongst others and with which the internal life, localized in the subject's own body, is contrasted

Corresponding to the early egocentricity in intellectual development at this stage, Piaget describes the affective states as attesting to 'a kind of general egocentricity [giving the impression] if one mistakenly attributes a sense of self to the baby, of a kind of love of self and of one's own activity' (Piaget, 1967, p. 16). And with the beginnings of the construction of an objective world comes the affective 'object choice' – some person, and eventually others, evoke responses.

With the second Pre-operational stage, the child acquires language. Now he or she begins to have access to the public world of shared meanings. However, the child's accommodation of others and of social reality is still limited because his or her thought is at this stage *intuitive*. By this Piaget means that while he or she may report perceptual experiences the child does not yet understand the activity of giving supporting reasons (either for belief or for action), so his or her use of language is mostly expressive (words have the form of avowals). The development of language use, like other forms of intellectual development, is a slow, attentuated process not complete, as we shall see, for some time.

Moreover, the child does not yet distinguish his or her own from another's point of view, so failing to value reasons (Piaget, 1967, p. 27):

> It is only *vis-à-vis* others that we are led to seek evidence for our statements. We always believe ourselves without further ado until we learn to consider the objections of others and to internalize such discussions in the form of reflection

In affective development the child exhibits 'interpersonal' emotions (affections, sympathies and antipathies) and learns to obey moral rules – although his or her morals remain *heteronomous* (that is, subject to the external will of the respected person or parents). Moral values then are also still *intuitive:* the child understands only that it is wrong to lie because it is against the (externally imposed) rules.

The loss of this continued egocentricity marks the new stage of Concrete Operations, which begins around the seventh year and is not completed until adolescence. Now the child learns to distinguish his or her own point of view and relate it to that of others. In doing so he or she also learns to entertain different points of view in consciousness, and to engage in internal debate (or what Piaget calls *reflection*) of the kind necessary for deliberate action. Thus the impulsive or intuitive action of the earlier stage appears less often.

Language becomes more fully communicative during this stage. Moreover, thought is no longer intuitive – a need is felt for a connection between ideas and logical justification (Piaget, 1967, p. 39). This, Piaget explains, is because the child has acquired the capacity for *reversibility* – for returning to the beginning of performances, both intellectual and practical. There is a parallel here with the ability, mentioned earlier, of adopting an objective point of view. Through reversibility the child develops an understanding of general concepts or classes, and now logic (defined as a system of relationships which permit the coordination of points of view corresponding to different individuals, as well as those which correspond to the successive precepts or intuitions of the same individual) (Piaget, 1967, p. 41), can begin. Causality, conservation, time, space and motion are gradually mastered and understood conceptually; they become general schemata of thought, rather than schemata of action or intuition (Piaget, 1967, p. 46).

Paralleling the development of logic is the development of cooperation and personal autonomy in the moral sphere. This new system of values, Piaget says, represents in the affective sphere, the equivalent of logic in the realm of intelligence (Piaget, 1967, p. 41). Now can begin the morality of cooperation and mutual respect wherein rules are no longer treated as being the product of an external will, but as the result of explicit and tacit accord (Piaget, 1967, p. 56).

With the final stage of Formal Operations, a level of abstract thought becomes possible. Logical operations hitherto restricted to concrete objects can now be performed on abstractions, like general ideas. The logic of propositions becomes possible, in contrast to the logic of relations, classes and number engendered by concrete operations. Gradually developing egocentric assimilation of abstractions gives way to the process of *accommodation*, and there is a reconciliation between formal thought and reality (Piaget, 1967, p. 64). In the moral sphere the self is further decentred, and ideals and standards come to dictate courses of action.

The first three of the four stages described above deserve special attention, for our inclinations to excuse have ceased to be reliable by the time the child reaches adolescence. The absence of reason is less marked, and we seem correspondingly less certain of the innocence of the wrongdoer.

In the early sensorimotor stage a child is without thought and action, as we understand those attributes, and communicates only marginally. Even in the second stage the earlier total egocentricity of infancy still lingers to a substantial degree. The child, as we have seen, does not have a full understanding of the world as objective and independent of his or her own experience, being unaware of central shared metaphysical concepts such as space, time and causality. Without objective thought about the world, the ability to distinguish appearance from reality cannot emerge. Thus, while language is present, at first it has not the same public or intersubjective quality as has later language. In many ways it seems more like the 'language' of the schizophrenic, described earlier, which reflects idiosyncratic and arbitrary associations and has no public edge. It has some communicative functions (it is, as Piaget points out, expressive, for example) but it hardly warrants the title *language* in the fullest sense.

Logical relations are not yet understood and the child is still incapable of standard modes of adult hypothetico-deductive reasoning.

In addition, the child neither offers nor sees the need to offer supporting reasons. As a consequence, his or her action is impulsive; the tools are not yet available for the kind of reflection required by what we regard as deliberate action.

Finally, the child does not understand what it is to decide to follow a rule, in the adult sense. The demands of a heteronomous will are obeyed, but he or she does not respond to the dictates of his or her own will, which would seem requisite for *voluntary* action.

Only in the next stage (Concrete Operations), which takes the child until adolescence to complete, do we see gradual mastery in most of these abilities. Acquisition of major metaphysical and logical concepts allows for decentring and this in turn means that language comes to be used as a public and communicative tool in the fullest way. Deliberate action develops with a relinquishing of the intuitive approach to experience. In the moral sphere, the notion of following a rule develops as some rules come to be reached by tacit agreement. Something like an adult notion of voluntary actions seems possible. The *point* of moral rules, we might say, comes to be recognized, and thus the point of morality, as its cooperate element develops.

That this development occurs in roughly the sequence described is not, as I remarked earlier, in doubt. Piaget's basic findings have been confirmed in subsequent studies. However, the fixed and immutable nature of these stages in their relation to maturation has recently been questioned, and some evidence has

been adduced which invites the notion that children think differently from sane adults merely because *they have less knowledge*
than do adults. As one discussion concludes (Carey, 1984):

> Developmental psychologists wish to account for the vari-
> ance in behaviour among populations of different ages . . .
> but by far the most important source of variation is in
> domain specific knowledge. Children know less than adults.
> Children are novices in almost every domain in which adults
> are experts

With a different education and experience then, a child aged 6
years might demonstrate the reasoning abilities which are now
associated with an 8-year-old.

While it casts Piaget's findings in a very different light, this
hypothesis does not appear to alter the broad claims I have been
making in this chapter, however. Children do think differently
from adults – for whatever reason – and while this is so their prerationality functions as an excuse for wrongdoing. Were there
increased exposure to 'domain-specific knowledge', then perhaps
children of an earlier age would cease to think differently from
adults and would cease to require or merit the special excuse they
presently enjoy. Only as long as they exhibit unreason, at whatever age, do children have an excuse for wrongdoing; why they
do so is, for jurisprudence, unimportant.

Piaget's account of the child's prerationality must be
approached in two ways. I shall explore the significance of parallels between the child's thought and that of the psychotic,
suggested by Piaget's account, and then compare it with the traditional legal understanding of exculpating irrationality discussed
in Chapter 9. Before turning to these two considerations, however, an additional remark must be made about children.

Older children, especially, often seem more reasonable than
Piaget's findings suggest, even granted that these stages describe
the average child only. We have difficulty recognizing the child
we know in some of his descriptions. Piaget himself has acknowledged this point but, as he rightly says, this seems to be because
practical considerations related to perception and action domi-
nate so much of our lives. In these respects, children reach mastery earlier. (Their schemata of action and perception develop
before the general schemata of thought, as he puts it.) Only close

examination and ingenious experimentation, as Piaget has shown, will reveal the depth of unreason in an older child's thought and action.

Children and the Insane

Let us now consider whether the similar principle of exculpating nonrationality, which lies beneath our impulse to excuse both in the case of the juvenile offender and in that of the deranged criminal, refers to the same kind of want of reason. If we find a similar unreason in the two different kinds of case – and it need only be similar, not identical – where there is a widespread impulse to excuse, then it seems likely that we are excusing, in each case, on the basis of that unreason.

In emphasizing the gradually developing shift of focus away from an egocentric, subjective and private orientation of the infant towards a decentred, public, reality-based orientation like that of the normal adult, Piaget's account of the development of thought is particularly germane to the way in which psychotic thought may be distinguished.

In the early egocentricity of the infant and young child there seems to be a direct parallel with the private world of the schizophrenic which we explored in Chapter 6. Linking two central features of psychotic experience (thought disorder and hallucination), we saw that there was an inability to distinguish purely subjective and idiosyncratic experiences and meanings from those which were shared – intersubjective and public reality. This very inability seems to be the one gradually transcended in the young child's process of decentring.

These parallels between psychotic and children's thought have not gone unnoticed. Recognizing a major qualitative difference between the thought processes exhibited by the very young and by psychotics alike on the one hand and by normal adults on the other, Freud (1915) described the latter as *primary process* thinking. In his metapsychology this was distinguished from the rational, secondary process thinking of (sane) adults in being the characteristic means of functioning of the unconscious mental system, while secondary process thinking characterized conscious processes. In addition to marking the distinction between the two processes, however, Freud proposed a theory of regression whereby the adult occasionally exhibits the more primitive thought patterns: in dreams, slips, humour and – most notably and persistently – in psychosis. Thus, on his analysis, the thought of the psychotic not only parallels that of the young child but is developmentally undifferentiated from it.

Central as it is to Freud's account of primary processes, the regression hypothesis will not be defended here. Parallels between the thought of children and the insane are confirmed by Freud's descriptive account of the distinction alone. We may acknowledge a parallel between the prerational thinking of a young child and a schizophrenic's thought disorder, or the 4-year-old's confusion between reality and fantasy and a psychotic's failure to 'test reality', without equating the two, or regarding the adult psychotic as regressed to earlier modes of thought. Freud's hypothesis is suggestive and appealing as an account of these parallels but it extends to the mechanisms behind the psychological and behavioural manifestations of madness with which I am not concerned.

Prerationality and the Legal Notion of Exculpating Nonreason

Piaget describes an extensive want of reason in the child, which persists until adolescence. His notion of prerationality comprises a set of features much more general and pervasive than the particular kinds of ignorance expressed in the legal concept of the guilty mind or tests for criminal insanity. The child's want of reason rests on a number of interrelated immaturities of affective as well as cognitive development.

We saw earlier that legal formulations concerning the exculpating want of reason which grounds our impulse to excuse youthful wrongdoers took a more general and a more particular expression. There was a narrow knowledge criterion which developed contemporaneously in insanity law. Here children were responsible if they had a guilty mind and thus lacked a particular kind of moral knowledge. But this account was shown to be inadequate to meet the breadth of our moral intuition to excuse. Children whom we would wish to excuse from blame may know right from wrong and may thus be said to have a guilty mind. Moreover, a broadening of the knowledge account introduced with M'Naghten's rule, so that a more general ignorance of the 'nature and quality' of the action undertaken is included, was still shown insufficient to allow the knowledge interpretation of the child's want of reason to match our intuitions to excuse.

Along with this narrow account, however, we saw that a broader notion was at play in which the child lacking reason, understanding, discretion, or control of his or her mind (*compos mentis*) had a more general incapacity or set of incapacities. Adopting this latter notion, I suggest that those incapacities – the details of which the law does not provide – might be interpreted as the ones which, as we just saw, Piaget describes as being overcome around adolescence: logical reasoning, reflective thought, fully communicative use of language, and deliberate and voluntary action.

Because of the range of features that Piaget's notion of pre-rationality exhibits, the legal account of the child's want of reason, centring on absence of knowledge of right and wrong, or on absence of knowledge of the nature and quality of the wrongful act, must be insufficient to capture it and we must turn to these hints of a broader notion. A child may know right from wrong, in some superficial sense, or the nature of some particular wrongful act, and yet rightly be judged as innocent on account of a want of reason, if he or she does not yet possess the adult ability to distinguish subjective from public experiences and meanings, or does not understand the principle of general causal reasoning. Indeed, without the latter abilities it follows from the interrelated nature of intellectual and affective development which Piaget represents that the child could not fully know right from wrong, nor fully understand the nature of a given action.

Again, for all his seeming cunning and malice, the 8-year-old boy who burnt barns, described by Blackstone, would have been something a good deal less than a fully mature thinker, and the 'cunning' and 'malice' themselves – like the moral knowledge described above – could only have been faint replicas of those attitudes as they are ascribed to adults. An attribution of both terms to adults presupposes the capacity for fully voluntary and deliberate action, on the one hand, and the most sophisticated form of mental deliberation which requires an understanding of the justifying role of reasons, on the other – all attributes which, if we are to accept Piaget's findings, would be wanting in an 8-year-old boy.

The introduction to the insanity law of the excusing condition of compulsion to supplement knowledge tests for criminal insanity may, as I have said, help to justify our intuition to excuse with some children. However, Piaget's discussion of the child's affective development suggests that the simple dichotomy between acting voluntarily and acting under compulsion will not prove a very useful one in this case. True, it is many years before a child's action is deliberate or voluntary enough to be classified as free, but there are many alternatives to acting freely, of which acting under compulsion – a sophisticated adult mode itself requiring deliberation – is only one. For a long time, it would seem, the child acts neither freely nor under compulsion.

Even the composite tests for exculpating irrationality, which include both the knowledge criteria expressed in M'Naghten's Rule and some control criterion, far from completely capture the notion, and only Piaget's account permits the expanded concept of exculpating nonrationality sufficient to ground our intuitions to excuse juvenile wrongdoers.

In order to formulate this concept of what might be called exculpating unreason, we may appeal to Piaget's own image for the processes of development. The infant is pictured as beginning in total egocentricity and gradually decentring, in a series of stages which is finally complete only at the end of childhood. With the completion of decentring comes the recognition that the adult world is a shared one: experiences, meanings and rules are public and intersubjective rather than subjective and idiosyncratic. The decentred adolescent can reason logically, think reflectively, use language fully communicatively and engage in deliberate and voluntary action.

Not only may we use Piaget's categories to build out the incomplete notion of general incapacity expressed in juvenile law in the way outlined above – where a want of understanding (judgement, discretion, etc.) includes the four major incapacities characteristic of the pre-adolescent child; in addition, we may appeal to these categories to show how more elaborate tests for criminal insanity might be developed, the better to capture that class of cases about which we have an impulse to excuse. Those characteristics associated with the child to whom responsibility is ascribed go beyond the narrow kinds of ignorance singled out in M'Naghten and the deficiencies marking the control tests.

Piaget's picture of the child's inability to reason logically, think reflectively, communicate fully and act voluntarily corresponds to the broad notion of exculpating unreason sketched in earlier chapters: a pervasive inability to hold and act upon sufficient reasons and to entertain consistent beliefs and desires. The logical and communicative deficiencies of the child invite errors of judgement: they preclude his or her forming beliefs and desires which are well grounded; the child's reflective and volitional immaturities affect his or her ability to act on sufficient reasons.

This formulation will not *completely* capture the class of juvenile and deranged wrongdoers whom we would excuse. But it does make some advance on traditional legal formulations, and I shall argue later that difficulties arising out of border-line cases and the moral border-line between culpability and the attribution of responsibility make it unlikely that any such complete formulation could be found.

Why do these forms of unreason exculpate? I have attempted to strengthen the case for exculpating unreason in the insane by appeal to a similar impulse – more entrenched perhaps, and more consistently felt, towards children. Before leaving this discussion, we need to look at how these impulses are grounded or supported, not only when they are felt towards the insane but also when they apply to children.

The impulses or moral intuitions we are concerned with here present themselves in different ways: as (1) the general belief that certain conditions (ignorance, compulsion and a want of reason) excuse; and as (2) the impulse to excuse in a particular case – for example, that of the boy whom Blackstone describes as having set fire to two barns.

Justification also may be approached in different ways. We might describe how the positive notion of agency carries with it some conditions concerning rationality, knowledge and voluntariness such that when those conditions are not met we are reluctant to credit full responsibility. As Aristotle seems to have recognized when he couched his discussion of moral responsibility negatively in the *Nichomachean Ethics* by analysing the conditions under which full agency would *not* be present rather than those in which it would be, a complete positive account of moral responsibility may be very difficult to furnish, and I shall not undertake one here. However, some general remarks do seem possible about the requirements for agent responsibility in terms of necessary, if not

sufficient, conditions relating to the issues we have been considering: a responsible agent acts knowingly, voluntarily and with a
certain quality and quantity of reason.

This claim seems unexceptional. The links are obvious: agency
conveys the notion of moral responsibility which in turn requires
the appropriate ascription of praise and blame. For it to be
appropriate to praise and blame, it is necessary for the agent to
have acted freely – or to have caused his or her action in a
particular way, in soft determinist terminology. Free action or
action caused in this particular way typically involves deliberation
and choice. Choosing one action over another requires an understanding of the nature and consequences of the action chosen and
of the alternative courses not chosen – that is, the use of reasoning.
Indeed, such a view can be teased out of Aristotle's own remarks
on responsibility in the *Nichomachean Ethics* and the *Eudemian
Ethics* (Irwin, 1980).

The above sketch of the notion of agent responsibility, while it
is not complete, is sufficient to show a grounding or justification
which could be offered for the impulses to excuse the insane and
children. It is perhaps true that a positive account of agent
responsibility will also rest, ultimately, on unjustifiable intuitions; but ostensibly, at least, this account can be appealed to in
providing a warrant for beliefs of the kind described in (1) and (2).

A second approach to justification would permit us to ground
the general intuition (that ignorance excuses, for example) by
appeal to our intuitive response to particular cases. We can
explain the claim that ignorance excuses as a kind of generalization
from many instances in which two features are present: the
wrongdoer was (1) ignorant in the required sense and was (2) the
subject of an impulse to excuse.

(There may be a certain circularity involved in this notion of
justification. Wrongdoers classified as ignorant in the inductive
generalization just described share other features in common as
well as their ignorance: shortness of stature, emotional imma-
turity and certain childish interests and concerns might all characterize the class of children whom we would wish to excuse
because of their ignorance. In order to show why ignorance is
singled out here in justifying our impulse to excuse it may be
necessary to return to our initial intuition that, in general, ignorance excuses.)

As the preceding discussions should indicate, the impulse to excuse due to ignorance, compulsion and unreason is grounded in the same way whether in relation to the insane or to children. Since it is perhaps more widespread and unquestioned in the case of children, the analogy has been presented as resting on that case.

There is another aspect to justification here. The presence of the same features excusing children and the insane lends support to our general belief that ignorance, compulsion and unreason constitute grounds for excuse in the way that disease, for example, does not.

Defenders of the medical analysis which I attacked earlier in this book might perhaps be construed as claiming that disease itself is an excusing condition whose presence is affirmed by our moral intuitions, but this position is unconvincing. There is not a wide variety of cases and situations in which diseases excuse; indeed, as we saw in Chapter 3, ordinary diseases like tuberculosis do not excuse and nor do organic brain disorders do so *as* diseases. Because we appeal to ignorance, compulsion and unreason as excuses in both children and the insane, it is plausible to speak of an intuition to excuse due to these conditions while implausible to speak of disease as an excuse.

11
The Insanity Plea

Some of the more practical applications of what has been until now a theoretical discussion will be looked at in this chapter. By re-examining the history of the legal use of insanity as a defence we shall see how, with increased emphasis on a medical understanding of madness, a change occurred in the legal concept of insanity as an excuse, which was reflected both in influential new formulations and tests for criminal insanity and in courtroom practices surrounding the plea's application. Law and practice came to rely on the assumption that diseases are excuses derived from the disease analogy and shown in Chapter 3 to be unwarranted.

I shall urge a return to a less medical way of viewing the insanity plea. Building on earlier discussion of insanity law and ways in which the traditional knowledge and control tests failed, I shall offer a formulation which appeals to the notion of exculpating unreason in order to make good some of these deficiencies. This will not be claimed as an exhaustive test which matches our moral intuitions in every case, however. I shall argue that such a test would be impossible to construct, since the very distinction between insanity which exculpates, on the one hand, and sane behaviour to which culpability attaches, on the other, lies on a moral border-line about which there is not complete agreement.

Finally, I shall argue that at some future time the medical model may have its rightful ascendancy – but only when our impulse to excuse no longer exists. If medical knowledge of the causes and cures of insanity were ever to put the procedures of prevention within the reach of the deranged, their condition would no longer count as an excuse.

Insufficiencies of Early Tests

To understand the problem raised by the increased medical influence on the insanity plea, it is necessary to return to the history of insanity as a defence in Anglo–American law, and to trace the sources of its current orientation.

Some of these historical details were set forth in Chapter 9. To recapitulate: after a history spanning back at least as far as the sixteenth century in which reference was made to *mens rea* (or the guilty mind) in explaining the condition the insane criminal failed to fulfil, a formal rule for criminal insanity was adopted in the middle of the nineteenth century. The central aspect of M'Naghten's Rule places stress on a want of reason resulting from a 'disease or defect of the mind' not permitting the accused to know, at the time of the act of wrongdoing, the 'nature and quality' of the act, or that it was wrong.

This rule was welcomed and adopted both in England and in most courts in the United States. Its benefit was twofold: it provided a criterion by which a jury might determine whether criminal responsibility was present in any given case. Moreover, in appealing to the traditional excusing condition of ignorance, M'Naghten provided a reason or justification for excusing the insane.

Some of the difficulties with this rule were also seen in Chapter 9. One of these was that severe insanity, of the kind we would wish to excuse, is not always manifested in a failure of the particular kind of knowledge there described. A solution to this difficulty was proposed with the introduction of control tests. Now persons were said to have an excuse not only if they did not know what they did but if, knowing it, they could not exercise the requisite control to refrain from doing it. Taken as a necessary condition for criminal insanity, however, the control tests failed to capture all of the class of deranged criminals our intuitions would encourage us to excuse: for instance, the brooding, deliberative – but deeply depressed – murderer. Even formulations in which ignorance and compulsion were treated separately as sufficient conditions for the ascription of exculpating insanity proved unable to capture all those we regard as severely disturbed.

Medical Influences on the Insanity Plea

By the 1950s another solution to these problems emerged and it was one which reflected the widespread acceptance of the disease analogy and of medical psychiatry. The Durham Rule (*Durham* v. *US*) proposed simply that the accused was not criminally responsible if his wrongful act was 'the product of mental disease or defect', when 'disease' is defined as a condition which is capable of improving or deteriorating and 'defect' as a condition not considered capable of improving or deteriorating. In his opinion, Judge Bazelon remarked that the fundamental objection to traditional knowledge tests

. . . is not that criminal irresponsibility is made to rest upon an inadequate, invalid or indeterminable symptom or manifestation, but that it is made to rest upon *any* particular symptom

By attempting to define insanity in terms of a symptom, he went on (p. 872);

The courts assumed an impossible role, not merely one for which they have no special competence . . . (it is dangerous to) abstract particular mental facilities, and to lay it down that unless these particular facilities are destroyed or gravely impaired, an accused person, whatever the nature of his mental disease, must be held to be criminally responsible. . . . In this field of law as in others, the fact finder should be free to consider all information advanced by relevant scientific disciplines (my parentheses added)

Because of its stark reliance upon the disease analogy and its medical presuppositions and overtones, Durham stands out among modern formulations which introduce such ideas. It was not, however, the first such formulation.[1] Considering these issues at the end of the nineteenth century, the state of New Hampshire avoided embracing M'Naghten's Rule or any knowledge or control test and instead relied upon a test for criminal insanity based only on the notion that diseases are excuses, just as Durham does. If the killing were the 'offspring or product of mental disease', it states, then the defendant should be acquitted (*State* v. *Pike*).

However, it is Durham rather than the New Hampshire law which deserves our particular attention and stands at the heart of these medical encroachments on the insanity plea. This is not because Durham has been extensively accepted. Its influence, in that sense, hardly goes beyond that of the New Hampshire Rule.[2] Rather, it is because coming half a century later Durham seems to have been a reflection of a widespread and pervasive informal acceptance of the disease analogy shaping practice and procedure which surrounded the insanity plea at the time it was formulated. By the 1950s the discipline of psychiatric medicine had developed to a point of unprecedented influence. Early successes with the use of chemical treatment permitted a confidence in the promise of treatment and cure for psychiatric conditions which has not been entirely realized in the 30 years that have followed. A sophisticated psychiatric nosology permitted at least the appearance of precision and scientific rigour to attach to the new knowledge of madness, and psychiatry had gained widespread popular recognition and acceptance as a branch of medicine. This period reflects the high water mark of medical psychiatry's influence, when it was unmarred by later attacks from the antipsychiatry movement.

Matching the Durham Rule, another indication of medical psychiatry's having thus come of age can be seen in the effects of a procedural development: the use of psychiatrists and psychologists as expert witnesses in trials where insanity was an issue. Gradually becoming more common and patterned on the adversarial system favoured in the USA, so that first the prosecution and then both defence and prosecution came to rely on such expert testimony,[3] the presence of the psychiatric expert in the courtroom is now commonplace. However, bringing psychiatry into the courtroom has had significant and unwelcome effects. It has resulted in whast one judge has described as 'the expert's stronghold on the process' (*US* v. *Brawner*, p. 1011), whereby the experts' technical language and conceptual scheme has eclipsed the moral and legal inquiry into the responsibility of the accused, and the experts themselves have usurped the jury's task of forming nontechnical opinions about the case. In courts using traditional knowledge and control tests these effects were attributed to the clashing conceptual systems of the two disciplines of psychiatry and law, and the problem of forcing medical claims into a legal framework. Although it was designed to eliminate this weakness, the 'product' formulation of Durham merely aggravated the fundamental problem, however. In the words of the *Brawner* case (p. 983), in which the *Durham* Rule was finally rejected,

> There is, indeed, irony in a situation under which the Durham rule, which was adopted in large part to permit experts to testify in their own terms concerning matters within their domain which the jury should know, resulted in testimony by the experts in terms not their own to reflect unexpressed judgments in a domain that is properly not theirs but the jury's. The irony is heightened when the judgments, instructed under the esoteric 'product' standard, are influenced significantly by 'product' testimony of expert witnesses really reflecting ethical and legal judgments rather than a conclusion within the witness's particular expertise

The general criticism of the role of psychiatric experts developed here has come to be recognized, not only by lawyers and opponents of medical psychiatry but also by psychiatrists themselves. Various proposals have been made to curb the role of the expert (American Psychiatric Association, 1982) and to distinguish the medical questions involved from legal and moral judgements on the so-called 'ultimate issues'. It remains to be seen whether these distinctions can be maintained in practice and such a curb on the influence of psychiatric experts effectively carried out.

With the adoption of Durham and greater reliance on psychiatric experts, the insanity plea has suffered increasing medical influence in the second half of the twentieth century, for each indicates an acceptance of the disease analogy underlying the medical model of madness criticized in previous chapters. Most naturally understood, Durham's wording implies that diseases as such excuse wrongdoing. It is possible, of course, to understand the key term 'product' in such a way as to avoid inconsistency with my position and with traditional legal notions of excuse: the causal link between mental disease or defect and act of wrongdoing may be taken to be mediated by 'symptoms' of ignorance and compulsion (or, more generally, unreason). However, this is at odds with the intent of Durham where the question for the jury is said to be (*Durham* v. *US*, pp. 875–6):

whether the accused acted because of a mental disorder, and not whether he displayed particular symptoms which medical science has long recognized do not necessarily, or even typically, accompany even the most serious mental disorder

Such interpretation would leave unexplained how Durham can be seen as an improvement upon the traditional knowledge and control tests for criminal insanity which came before it. For they also emphasized that the ignorance and compulsion of the insane defendant must be the outcome of a disease or defect of the mind. The advantage claimed for Durham rests on interpreting the 'product' formulation as asserting that mental diseases as such serve to excuse the wrongdoer.

The increased use of psychiatric experts has seemed to suggest the same dubious assumption and to hint at another one: that whether the accused ought to be excused is an empirical question. The latter presupposition is equally unwarranted. Whether or not some brain dysfunction was present and influenced the criminal act, the nonscientific question remains. Was the accused morally responsible? Should he or she be blamed or excused? This is not a question which the members of a lay jury are in any way insufficiently equipped to answer, possessing as they can be expected to do, common sense, a knowledge of character, an understanding of the meaning of plain words and a sense of what is just and fair. Nor is it a question to which the psychiatric experts' particular expertise could give them any privileged claim.

A Solution

It was in order to solve a problem that Durham introduced the unwarranted assumption that diseases as such serve to excuse wrongdoing. Neither knowledge tests based on M'Naghten's Rule nor a formulation combining knowledge and control tests were adequate to cover all the cases of derangement towards which there are agreed upon moral intuitions to excuse. With my rejection of the disease analogy solution adopted in Durham the problem reappears.

A partial solution was sketched in the earlier chapters of this book. I have been arguing that while diseases as such are not excuses, a certain kind of unreason does serve to excuse, just as ignorance and compulsion traditionally have been regarded as so doing. The notion of exculpating unreason developed in previous chapters has been defined as a pervasive inability to hold and act upon sufficient reasons and to avoid holding inconsistent beliefs and desires. My proposal is that a certain kind of irrationality lessens responsibility and that our intuition to excuse some of the insane criminals recalcitrant to traditional knowledge and control criteria may be justified by appeal to their want of reason.

We must now consider how this conclusion might be introduced into legal formulations concerning insanity as a defence. We have seen the way in which the excusing conditions of ignorance and compulsion are built into tests for criminal insanity. I argued that, even if we appeal to the broadest possible reading of knowledge tests such as M'Naghten's, we still lose cases of lessened responsibility which could be captured by appeal to exculpating unreason.

Much of the dissatisfaction with a medical notion of criminal insanity sketched in the previous section of this chapter has been acknowledged in the last few years and a more cautious and conservative attitude towards the use of the insanity plea is found reflected not only in legal but also in psychiatric discussions. I shall concentrate on one important example of this trend: the model statute drafted by the Institute of Law, Psychiatry and Public Policy at the University of Virginia – the so-called Bonnie Rule. The Bonnie Rule has been recommended not only by lawyers but also by the American Psychiatric Association. In a statement issued in 1982 (p. 12) it is asserted that this Rule, 'is the one which the American Psychiatric Association believes does permit relevant psychiatric testimony to be brought to bear on the great majority of cases where criminal responsibility is at issue'.

The Bonnie Rule states that a person charged with a criminal offence

. . . should be found not guilty by reason of insanity if it is shown that as a result of mental disease or mental retardation he was unable to appreciate the wrongfulness of his conduct at the time of the offense

when

As used in this standard, the terms mental disease or mental retardation include only those severely abnormal mental conditions that grossly and demonstrably impair a person's perception or understanding of reality and that are not attributable primarily to the voluntary ingestion of alcohol or other psychoactive substances

What is most notable about this rule is that like M'Naghten's it contains no reference to control – it is a knowledge test only. In discussing this omission the American Psychiatric Association (1982, p. 12) has argued that reference to the control element would have been redundant:

> Most psychotic persons who fail a volitional test for insanity will also fail a cognitive-type test when such a test is applied to their behavior, thus rendering the volitional test superfluous in judging them

Since psychosis is usually defined in terms of the 'cognitive' failure of reality testing, this claim seems indisputable. However, I would insist that the case of the nonpsychotic kleptomaniac ought to be excused, on the grounds that while not psychotic the kleptomaniac's inability to refrain from stealing is a psychological disability of the kind described here as exculpating unreason.

The Bonnie Rule has several other drawbacks. Its use of the phrase 'mental disease' suggests a reliance on the disease analogy which I have shown in this book to be unwarranted; moreover, it raises the problem of an adequate definition for the term – although the one it provides goes far towards overcoming that omission in previous formulations which introduce the expression. More important, however, is the narrowing of the knowledge or 'appreciation' criterion with the omission of M'Naghten's 'nature and quality' phrase. Broadly interpreted, we saw in Chapter 9, that phrase captures several kinds of case which it is our impulse to excuse and which are excluded by a simple moral knowledge criterion. The Bonnie Rule is too narrow to encompass several cases of severe derangement which not only fit its own definition of mental disease (as severely abnormal mental conditions that grossly and demonstrably impair a person's perception and understanding of reality) but also require the use of insanity as a defence according to widespread moral attitudes.

Because of these difficulties with Bonnie, I suggest not a gloss on it but a new test. In order to capture the broader interpretation of knowledge tests for which I have been arguing as well as the position developed in this book that a certain kind of unreason counts as an excuse, I would propose the following broader, all-encompassing test for criminal insanity:

persons charged with a criminal offense should be found not guilty by reason of insanity if it is shown that their act resulted either from a pervasive defect of mind manifested in their not holding and acting upon sufficient reasons or not holding consistent beliefs and desires,[4] or an inability to control their actions

Border-line Cases and Moral Border-lines

Caution is required here. As has long been recognized, the point at which insanity is sufficient to require special status for its sufferer is an elusive one. In the words of a nineteenth-century case concerning testamentary capacity (*Boyse* v. *Rossborough*),

There is no difficulty in the case of a raving madman or of a drivelling idiot, in saying that he is not a person capable of disposing of his property. But between such an extreme case and that of a man of perfectly sound and vigorous understanding, there is every shade of intellect, every degree of mental capacity. There is no possibility of mistaking midnight for noon; but at what precise moment twilight becomes darkness is hard to determine

I have dealt with only a few of the major kinds of psychiatric disorder: those distinguished by their severity (psychotic states, paranoia and affective disorders in their more extreme form). There are also many less severe disturbances as well, and it is frequently the sufferers of such disorders who pose the greatest difficulty for the legal use of insanity as a defence, because they strain both our moral intuition and the tests for criminal insanity. The impulse to excuse the insane wrongdoer is not universal, of course, but away from the agreed upon central cases, disagreement and uncertainty arise even among those moved by the general conviction that insanity is an excuse. Somewhere on the border-line between sane and deranged, we *all* lose our impulse to exculpate. Introducing unreason as an excusing condition will enable us to ground our intuition to excuse in the case of the more severe disorders, and advances us further than the criteria of ignorance and compulsion as they are interpreted in traditional tests. However, it will not help us draw a net around all those whom we would be inclined to excuse.

No such excusing condition could be found, however, and no such corresponding test for exculpating insanity constructed. Exculpating insanity is itself a concept extremely imprecise in its application, with vague border-lines over which there is real disagreement. No test for criminal insanity could completely capture a concept whose application is so problematic.

My position here is not to be confused with a view sometimes adopted concerning the so-called uncertainty of law (Black, 1974): that unresolved legal questions result from a failure of authoritative materials (precedents, statutes and constitutional provisions) to yield any one 'correct' answer to many close questions of law, so that legal decisions reflect the personal attitudes of judges rather than a 'true' answer derived from the body of law itself. It is not the uncertainty introduced by *any* appeal to a subjective element with which I am concerned. Rather, it is with the particular kind of uncertainty which results from a failure of agreement and judgement on certain contested moral issues. In the case of many issues the judge's moral intuitions, though subjective, would prove to be clearcut and reflective of agreed-upon societal attitudes and beliefs.

Some courts have attempted to respond to the problem of inexactness raised here by introducing the notion of diminished responsibility.[5] Part of what troubles us over these border-line cases can be dealt with in this way. Those who are sane, on the one hand, and psychotic, on the other, appear to stand at either end of a continuum upon which degrees of responsibility can be nicely mapped. The puzzling cases in the middle seem neither entirely sane – and so fully culpable – nor entirely insane – and so excusable. They may rightly be said to reflect diminished responsibility.

But to suppose the problem of vagueness entirely resolved by according degrees of responsibility would be mistaken. We are as confused over where to begin ascribing some given degree of culpability as we are when to ascribe sanity and insanity. It is a moral border-line: the moral concept of exculpating insanity itself is soft-edged in its application. At its boundaries, intuitions break down or falter. Serious and thoughtful people disagree – and simply do not know what is right in these cases.

The law deals with other areas, it is true, in which such moral border-lines arise. The one most analogous is perhaps the great question of juvenile justice – when does a young person reach adult culpability? We know children are not rightly held morally responsible, while adults are, but people lose their own sense of what is just over the vague area of youth between those two clear categories.

Similar to this is the question of fetal rights. For many moderates, at least, there is a point somewhere between conception and birth when it becomes appropriate to accord the fetus a right to life. Where the line must be drawn, however, is not easy to decide; the moral concept of personhood is vague and here, too, moral intuitions falter.

In both the case of juvenile responsibility and in that of fetal rights there are objective points at which a line may be drawn to establish a criterion defined by concepts themselves neutral enough to quiet endless interpretation. Most obvious of these is chronological age. At age 16 (in certain states and for certain crimes) the law has declared, the juvenile acquires adult culpability; at the end of the second trimester the fetus acquires a right to life. Though arbitrary, a rule can be established by appeal to this objective standard, and courtroom disputes and confusion of the kind which bedevil attempts to prove exculpating insanity can be avoided.

Such an arbitrary assigning of a standard is not, of course, without difficulties. That the confusion remains in our minds, and with it a sense of the unsatisfactorily blunt quality of such sharply drawn boundaries, must not be underestimated. Indeed, the uneasy feel of a moral border-line is perhaps more strongly present when such sharp boundaries are introduced than it is when the ambiguities of terms like 'know', 'control' and 'impulse' can serve to conceal and soften differences of opinion. However, the possibility of its resolution *in the courtroom*, nevertheless marks off these issues of juvenile culpability and fetal rights from the moral border-line between guilt and exculpating insanity.

In contrast to these sharp lines, the tests for exculpating

insanity must appeal to concepts like 'know' and 'control'. There are, granted, objective tests for present ignorance and compulsion comparable to the chronological standard. A behavioural criterion could be used, for example, such that knowing a proposition is defined as the ability to give assent to it. Similar behavioural tests for compulsion have been proposed, though sometimes ironically, as in the case of Baron Bramwell's Rule whereby a person is compelled to do an (illegal) action if that person would do it even aware of a policeman at his or her elbow (Foster and Finlason's Nisi Prius Cases, 1859). These tests have the bluntness of the chronological age test described earlier.

However, in the case of insanity as a defence, it is not the present state of mind of the accused which is under consideration, but a past state of mind, and it is not at all clear what could count as present indication of a past behavioural tendency like those described. How could we prove that a person knew something or acted compulsively *in the past?* Only indirectly and uncertainly at best. In their application these concepts have none of the hardness of the concept of chronological age; they are soft, vague and open to interpretation.[6]

So the issue of exculpating insanity presents a special case; there is a radical uncertainty surrounding the concept's application which seems irresolvable. This means that no test for criminal insanity will be sufficient to deal with every case. Whatever criteria are adopted will inevitably be severely strained by puzzle cases. [A somewhat similar conclusion to this one is found in *Holloway* v. *US* (1945): 'The application of these tests (M'Naghten and irresistible impulse), however they are phrased, to a borderline case can be nothing more than a moral judgement that it is just or unjust to blame the defendant for what he did'.]

Medical Psychiatry's Ascendancy

I have spoken of the dubious claim that diseases are excuses as a flaw in the medical model of madness, yet in one way it is more than that. Were the medical model to triumph and to realize the expectations its adherents profess, then we could expect the decline of the very moral intuition which, I have argued, that model cannot accommodate. For the intuition itself appears to be dependent on the present imperfect state of medical knowledge.

Treatment, and certainly cure, in psychiatry today, are unreliable. In a field where there is such fundamental disagreement as to the causes of the conditions observed and such complexity to the phenomena involved, this is not, perhaps, surprising. If we accept the optimistic predictions of theorists, who promise that advances in knowledge of brain science and chemistry soon will reveal the underlying physical basis of human motivation and behaviour, it would seem that we will eventually be entitled to a greater confidence.

Let us suppose that it will be possible, some day, to cure the disturbed criminal routinely upon apprehension. Already there are temporary cures of this kind: a florid psychotic state can often be quelled by the use of drugs. We can imagine treatment and finally a permanent cure coming routinely to precede formal sentencing in the way that a psychiatric examination does today.[7]

Were this so, however, critical changes might also be expected to have taken place in the moral dimensions of the situation.

Were cures known and available for psychiatric conditions, then individuals might come to be regarded as responsible for their state and perhaps even for the mental state of those around them. If a person were to be held responsible for his or her mental state, it would seem to follow that such a person would also be held responsible for wrongdoing undertaken because of that state.

There would now be a closer parallel between the crimes of the artificially cured and crimes induced by alcohol and drugs. We hold the criminal responsible for wrongful actions undertaken under the influence of such toxic substances (given certain qualifications) because he or she could have avoided the occasion of crime, as we saw earlier. Similarly, it might be said, the deranged criminal could have been expected to have sought a cure prior to the occasion of wrongdoing and perhaps even sought reassurance as to his or her mental state in order to ascertain the need for such a cure. Thus the deranged criminal also would probably be held culpable for his or her wrongdoing. Our intuitions concerning psychiatric medicine would be no different from those concerning ordinary physical medicine if this were so. As we saw earlier, to the extent that medical knowledge can offer preventive procedures, we already temper our sympathy for the sufferer of a physical ailment.

Were this day to dawn, the medical model would have completely arrived – but, by then, insanity would not rightly count as an excuse. At such a time – and only then – I insist, would a medical model be appropriate in moral and legal thinking about madness.

Notes

1 Nor is it the last. The verdict introduced by the State of Oregon has the defendant not responsible by reason of disease or defect, for example.
2 Although much discussed, the Rule has only been adopted in a handful of courts.
3 Two decades ago only 3 percent of criminal cases had counterposed prosecution and defence experts, for example (Jenkins, 1983).
4 This wording is meant to allow that the fundamental defect does not *always* manifest itself in either of these ways (acting upon insufficient reasons and holding inconsistent beliefs and desires).
5 First developed in Scottish Law, this principle was adopted in the British Homicide Act (1957) and, more recently, in California. As is indicated by its recent abolition in California, however (Calif. Penal Code, 1981) it is not without its critics.
6 In one way, this objection applies to all questions of *mens rea* since the prosecution is required to establish that the accused acted with intent (a mental state) at the time of the crime (in the past). However, the concept of *mens rea* is not itself on a moral border-line over which there is consistent disagreement between thinking people: it certainly raises puzzles because of its obscurity, but they are not moral puzzles.
7 The practice of establishing 'chemical sanity' before trial raises important questions of personal identity and responsibility and has rightly been questioned. These concerns may prevail and the scenario I describe may never come to be. My only point is that, if it does, then so may the consequences I have sketched here.

References

American Law Institute (1955), *Model Penal Code*, Section 4.01.

American Psychiatric Association, *Diagnostic and Statistical Manual of Mental Disorders* (DSM III) Third Edition (American Psychiatric Association, Washington DC, 1980).

American Psychiatric Association (1980), *Glossary of Diagnostic and Statistical Manual*, 3rd edn (Boston: Little Brown & Co.).

American Psychiatric Association (1982), *Statement on the Insanity Defense*, (Washington DC: American Psychiatric Association).

Aristotle, *Nichomachean Ethics*, trans. W. D. Ross in R. McKeon (ed.) *The Basic Works of Aristotle* (New York, Random House, 1941).

Aristotle, *Eudemian Ethics*, in J. Barnes, *The Complete Works of Aristotle, The Revised Oxford Translation* (Princeton University Press, 1984).

Austin, J. L. (1956–7), 'A Plea for Excuses', *Proceedings of the Aristotelian Society*, reprinted in J. Urmson and G. Warnock (eds) *J. L. Austin: Philosophical Papers* (1970) Oxford University Press. [Page references are to this edition.]

Bates, E. (1977), *Models of Madness* (St. Lucia, Queensland: University of Queensland Press).

Beck, A. T. (1967), *Depression: Clinical, Experimental and Theoretical Aspects* (New York, Hoeber).

Beck, A. T. (1974), 'The Development of Depression: A Cognitive Model' in Friedman, R. J. and Katz, M. M. (eds) *The Psychology of Depression: Contemporary Theory and Research* (Washington DC: Winston).

Beck, A. T. (1976), *Cognitive Therapy and the Emotional Disorders* (New York: International Universities Press).

Beck, A. T. (1978), *Rush, Shaw and Emery, Cognitive Theories of Depression* (University of Pennsylvania Press).

Black, C. L. (1974), *Capital Punishment: The Inevitability of Caprice and Mistake* (New York: Norton).

Blackstone, W. (1765–7), *Commentaries on the Laws of England* (London), a facsimile of the First Edition (University of Chicago Press, 1970).

Bonnie, J. R. (1982), *A Model Statute on the Insanity Defense*, (Institute of Law, Psychiatry and Public Policy, University of Virginia).

Boorse, C. (1975), 'On the Distinction between Disease and Illness', *Philosophy and Public Affairs*, vol. 5, pp. 49–68.

Boyse v. *Rossborough*, 6 H.L. Cas. 2, 45, 10 Eng. Rep. 1192, 1210 (1857).

Brown, R. (1973), 'Schizophrenia, Language and Reality', *American Psychologist*, pp. 395–403.

Brown, R. (1976), 'Psychosis and Irrationality' in Benn, S. I. and Mortimor, G. W. (eds), *Rationality and the Social Sciences: Contributions to the philosophy and methodology of the social sciences* (London: Routledge).

Burton, R. (1621), *The Anatomy of Melancholy* 11th edn (London: J. E. Hodson, 1806).

167

168   Madness and Reason

Cameron, N. (1963), *Personality Development and Psychopathology* (Boston: Houghton Mifflin Co.).

Card, C. (1972), 'Mercy and Forgiveness', *Philosophical Review*, vol. 81, pp. 182–207.

Carey, S. (1984), 'Are Children Fundamentally Different Kinds of Thinkers and Learners than Adults?' in Chipman, S., Segal, J. and Glaser, R., *Thinking and Learning Skills: vol. 2* (Boston: Erlbaum Associates).

Carstairs, G. M. (1959) 'The Social Limits of Eccentricity' in Opler, M. K. (ed.), *Culture and Mental Health* (New York: Macmillan).

Clegley, H. (1950), *The Mask of Sanity*, 2nd edn (St Louis: Mosby & Co.).

Commonwealth v. *Rogers*, 48 Mass 500 (1844).

Coulter, J. (1973), *Approaches to Insanity: A Philosophical and Anthropological Study* (New York: Wiley).

Crowcroft, A. (1967), *The Psychotic: Understanding Madness* (London: Penguin).

Culver, G. and Gert, C. (1982), *Philosophy and Medicine* (Oxford University Press, London).

Custance, J. (1952), *Wisdom, Madness and Folly: The Philosophy of a Lunatic* (New York: Pellegrini & Cudahy).

Daniel M'Naghten's Case, 10c and F200, 210–11, 8 Eng. Rep. 718, 722–3 (1843).

Davis v. *US*, 165 US 373, 378 (1897).

Dubos, R. (1971), *The Mirage of Health* (New York: Harper & Row).

Durham v. *US*, 214F 2nd 862 (DC circ. 1954).

Edwards, R. (1982), 'Mental Health as Rational Autonomy' in Edwards, R., *Psychiatry and Ethics* (New York: Prometheus Books).

Feinberg, J. (1970) 'What is So Special about Mental Illness?' in Feinberg, J., *Doing and Deserving* (Princeton University Press).

Feinstein, A. (1967), *Clinical Judgment* (Baltimore: Williams & Wilkins).

Fingarette, H. (1967), *The Meaning of Criminal Insanity* (University of California Press).

Flew, A. (1975), *Crime or Disease?* (London: Macmillan).

Foster and Finlason's Nisi Prius Cases, 666,667 (1859).

Foucault, M. (1961), *Folie et Déraison: Histoire de la Folie* (Paris: Libraire Plon) [Page references are to *Madness and Reason* (trans. Howard) (New York: Random House, 1965)].

Foucault, M. (1963), *Naissance de la Clinique* (Paris: Presses Universitaire de France); *The Birth of the Clinic* (trans. Sheridan Smith) (New York: Random House, 1973).

Freud, S. (1900), *The Interpretation of Dreams* [Page references to 1965 edition (New York: Avon Books)].

Freud, S. (1915), 'The Unconscious', first published in *Zeitschrift* Bd III; reprinted in *Freud: General Psychological Theory* (New York: Collier Books, 1963).

Freud, S. (1917), 'Mourning and Melancholia' in *Collected Papers* (London: Hogarth Press, 1957).

Gardner, H. (1974), *The Shattered Mind* (New York: Random House).

Goldstein, A. (1967), *The Insanity Defense* (Yale University Press).

Gross, H. (1978), *The Psychological Society* (New York: Random House).

Hare R. M. (1963) *Freedom and Reason* (Oxford University Press).

Holloway v. *US*, 80 US App. DC 3, 4, 148 F 2d 665, 666 (1945).

Hoover v. *State*, 161 Ind. 384, 393, 68 NE 591, 593 (1903).

In Re Gault Supreme Court of US (1967), 387 US 87 S Ct 1428 18L Ed 2nd 527.

Irwin, T. H. (1980), 'Reason and Responsibility in Aristotle' in Rorty, A. (ed.), *Essays on Aristotle's Ethics* (University of California Press, 1980).

James, T. E. (1960), 'The Age of Majority', *The American Journal of Legal History* (Philadelphia, Temple University School of Law Publications: American Society of Legal History, vol. 4).

Jenkins, J. (1983), 'The Expert's Day in Court', *New York Times Magazine*, Dec. 11.

Kenny, A. (1963), *Action, Emotion and Will* (London: Routledge & Kegan Paul).

Kraepelin, E. (1904), *Lectures in Clinical Psychiatry* (New York: Hafner Publishing Co.) [Page references to 1968 edn.]

Laing, R. D. (1959), *The Divided Self* (London: Tavistock) [Page references to 1965 edn (London: Penguin)].

Laing, R. D. (1961), *The Self and Others* (London: Tavistock).

Laing, R. D. and Esterson, A. (1964), *Sanity, Madness and the Family* (London: Tavistock).

Lambard, W. (1581), *Eirenarcha, or the Office of the Justices of Peace* (London: Ra. Newbery and H. Bynneman).

Lee v. *State*, 93 So 2d. 757, 760 (Ala.1957).

Linde, D. (1976) *Murder and Madness* (San Francisco: San Francisco Book Co.).

Low, P., Jeffries, J. and Bonnie, R. (1982), *Criminal Law* (New York: Foundation Press).

McCune v. *State*, 156 Tex. Cn R 207, 211, 240 S.W. 2nd 305, 308 (1951).

MacDonald, M. (1977), 'The Inner Side of Wisdom: Suicide in Early Modern England' *Psychological Medicine*, vol. 7.

Maher, B. (1966), *Principles of Psychopathology: An Experimental Approach* (New York: McGraw-Hill).

Maher, B. (1972), 'The language of schizophrenia: A review and interpretation', *British Journal of Psychiatry*, vol. 120, pp. 3–17.

Margolis, J. (1976), 'The Concept of Disease', *Journal of Philosophy and Medicine*, vol. 3, pp. 238–55.

Middelfort, H. C. E. (1981), 'Madness and Civilization in Early Modern Europe', in B. Malamont (ed.), *After the Reformation: Essays in Honor of J. H. Hexter* (University of Pennsylvania Press).

Moore, M. (1975), Some Myths about 'Mental Illness', *Archives of General Psychiatry*, vol. 32, pp. 1483–97.

Moore, M. (1980), 'Legal Conceptions of Mental Illness' in Brody, B. and Engelhardt, H. T. (eds), *Mental Illness: Law and Public Policy* (Boston: D. Reidel Publishing Co.).

Osmond, H. and Seigler, M. (1973), 'Aescalapian Authority', *The Hastings Center Studies*, vol. 2.

Osmond, H. and Seigler, M. (1974), *Models of Madness: Models of Medicine* (New York: Harper and Row).

Parsons, T. (1951), *The Social System* (Illinois: The Free Press).

Parsons v. *State*, 2 So. 854, 866–7 (Ala, 1887).

Pavey, D. (1968), 'Verbal behaviour in schizophrenia: a review of recent studies', *Psychological Bulletin*, vol. 70.

Pears, D. F. (1962), 'Causes and Objects of Some Feelings and Psychological Reactions', *Ratio*, vol. 4, reprinted in Hampshire, S. (ed.), *Philosophy of Mind* (New York: Harper & Row, 1966), pp. 143–69.

People v. *Pico*, 62 Cal 50, 54 (1882).

People v. *Schmidt*, 213 NY 324, 110 NE 945 (1915).

Piaget, J. (1948), *The Moral Judgement of the Child* (London: Routledge & Kegan Paul).

Piaget, J. (1953), *The Origin of Intelligence in the Child* (London: Routledge & Kegan Paul).

Piaget, J. (1967), *Six Psychological Studies* (New York: Random House).

Pies, R. (1979), 'On Myths and Countermyths', *Archives of General Psychiatry*, vol. 36, reprinted in Vatz, R. and Weinberg, L., *Thomas Szasz: Primary Values and Major Contentions* (New York: Prometheus, 1983).

Pinel, P. (1806), *A Treatise on Insanity* (New York: Hafner, 1962; facsimile of the first English edition).

Powell v. *Texas*, 392 US 514 (1968).

Radden, J. (1982), 'Diseases as Excuses: Durham and the Insanity Plea', *Philosophical Studies*, vol. 42, pp. 349–62.

Ray, I. (1860), *A Treatise on the Medical Jurisprudence of Insanity*, 4th edn. (Boston: Little Brown & Co.).

Regina v. *Townley*, 3 Fost. and F. 839, 847, 156 Eng. Rep. 384, 387 (1863).

Rosen, H. (1980), *The Development of Sociomoral Knowledge* (Columbia University Press).

Royal Commission on Capital Punishment, 1949–53, Report 131 (Cmd.8932). (London: HMSO, 1953).

Sanders, W. (ed.) (1970), *Juvenile Offenders for 1000 Years* (University of North Carolina Press).

Sarason, I. and Sarason, B. (1980), *Abnormal Psychology*, 3rd edn (New Jersey: Prentice Hall).

Schwartz, S. (ed.) (1978), *Language and Cognition in Schizophrenia* (New York: Wiley).

Sechehaye, M. (1951), *Autobiography of a Schizophrenic Girl* (New York: Grune & Stratton), reprinted in Kaplan, B. (ed.), *The Inner World of Mental Illness* (New York: Harper & Row, 1964) [Page references are to the 1964 edition).

Seeman, M. V. (1970), 'Analysis of psychotic language: a review and synthesis', *Diseases of the Nervous System*, vol. 31, pp. 92–9.

Shope, R. K. (1967), 'The psychoanalytic theories of wish-fulfillment and meaning', *Inquiry*, vol. 10, pp. 421–38.

Sigwick, P. (1973), 'Illness – Mental and Otherwise', *Hastings Center Studies*, vol. I.

Smart, A. (1968), 'Mercy', *Philosophy*, pp. 345–59.

Solomon, R. (1977), *The Passions* (New York: Doubleday).

Sprenger, J. and Kraemer, H. (1486), *Malleus Malificarum*.

State v. *Bundy*, 24 SC 439, 445 (1885).

State v. *Jones*, 50 NH 369, 434 (1871).

State v. *Pike*, 49 NH 399, 444, (1870).

Stephen, Sir James (1883), *History of the Criminal Law of England* (London: Macmillan).

Stone, L. (1982), 'Madness', *New York Review of Books*, December, pp. 28–36.

Szasz, T. (1961), *The Myth of Mental Illness* (New York: Hoeber-Harper).

Szasz, T. (1983), 'Major Contentions' in Vatz, R. and Weinberg, L. (ed.), *Thomas Szasz: Primary Values and Major Contentions* (New York: Prometheus).

Thalberg, I. (1964), 'Emotion and Thought', *American Philosophical Quarterly*, vol. 1, reprinted in Hampshire, S. (ed.), *Philosophy of Mind* (New York: Harper & Row, 1966), pp. 201–25.

US v. *Brawner*, 471 F 2d. 969 (1972).

Veatch, R. M. (1973), 'The Medical Model: Its Nature and Problems', *Hastings Center Studies*, vol. 1, reprinted in Edwards, R. (ed.), *Psychiatry and Ethics* (New York: Prometheus Books, 1982) [Page references are to the 1982 edition).

Virchow, R. (1858), *Cellular pathology as based upon physiological and pathological histology*, 2nd German edn, translated by Frank Chance (New York: Dover, 1971).

Von Domarus, E. (1944), 'The specific laws of logic in schizophrenia' in Kasanin, L. (ed.), *Language and Thought in Schizophrenia* (University of California).

Walker, D. P. (1982), *Unclean Spirits: Possession and Exorcism in France and England in the late Sixteenth and Early Seventeenth Centuries* (University of Pennsylvania Press).

Weyer, J. (1563), *De Praestigiis Daemonum* (Basel: Oporinus).

Williams, E. B. (1959), 'Belief and Pleasure' *Proceedings of the Aristotelian Society*, vol. XXXIII (Supplementary Volume), reprinted in Hampshire, S. (ed.), *Philosophy of Mind* (New York: Harper & Row, 1966, pp. 225–42).

Williams, E. B. (1964), 'Deductive reasoning in schizophrenia' *Journal of Abnormal Psychology*, pp. 47–61.

Windmiller, M., Lambert, N. and Turiel, E. (1980), *Moral Development and Socialization* (Boston: Allyn & Bacon, Inc.).

Wittgenstein, L. (1953), *Philosophical Investigations* (Oxford: Blackwell).

Zilboorg, G. and Henry, G. (1941), *A History of Medical Psychology* (New York: Norton & Co.).

Index

172